Celtic Ireland
West of the River Shannon

Celtic Ireland West of the River Shannon

A Look Back at the Rich Heritage
And Dynastic Structure of the Gaelic
Clans

Patrick Lavin

*Illustrations Prepared by
Edith W. Lavin*

Writers Club Press
New York Lincoln Shanghai

Celtic Ireland West of the River Shannon
A Look Back at the Rich Heritage And Dynastic Structure of the Gaelic Clans

All Rights Reserved © 2003 by Patrick Lavin

No part of this book may be reproduced or transmitted in any form or by any means, graphic, electronic, or mechanical, including photocopying, recording, taping, or by any information storage retrieval system, without the written permission of the publisher.

Writers Club Press
an imprint of iUniverse, Inc.

For information address:
iUniverse, Inc.
2021 Pine Lake Road, Suite 100
Lincoln, NE 68512
www.iuniverse.com

Cataloging-In-Publication Data available from the Library of Congress.

1. Ireland—Celtic—prehistoric—historic.
2. Ireland—mythical—pre-Christian—Heroic Age.
3. Ireland—early Christian—medieval—colonial.
4. Ireland—Connacht—tribes—clans—families.
5. Ireland—Vikings—Anglo-Normans—Anglo-Irish.

Every reasonable effort has been made to trace the owners of copyright material in this book, but in some instances this has proven impossible. The author and publisher will be pleased to receive information leading to more complete acknowledgements in subsequent prints, and, in the meantime, extend their apologies for any omissions.

ISBN: 0-595-26477-8

Printed in the United States of America

*For my daughter,
Edie Lavin*

Contents

Introduction xiii

Chapter 1   Beyond the Mists. 3
- *The Mesolithic Period (8000–4000 B.C.)* 4
- *The Neolithic Period (4000–2000 B.C.)* 4

Chapter 2   Emergence of Celtic Ireland 11
- *Medieval Versions of Celtic Incursions* 12
- *The First Wave—Priteni Colonists* 12
- *The Second Wave—Euerni Colonists* 13
- *Third Wave—Laginian Colonists* 14
- *The Last Wave—Milesians (Gaels)* 15
- *Summary* 15

Chapter 3   The Mythical Tradition. 17
- *Summary* 21

Chapter 4   Early Celtic Ireland 25
- *Recurring Power Struggles* 27
- *The Emergence of the Midlands Connachta Dynasty* 29
- *Social Structure of Pre-Christian Ireland* 30

Chapter 5   Religion. 35
- *Druidism* 35
- *Christianity* 37
- *The Rise of the Ascetic Celi De* 41

Chapter 6   Medieval Ireland 47
- *Viking Invasion* 47

- Post-Viking Period *51*
- Anglo-Norman Invasion *52*
- Structure of Norman-Irish Society *54*
- The Medieval Church in Ireland *55*
- Climatic Changes and Calamities. *57*
- Colonial Retrogression Sets In. *58*

CHAPTER 7   Ancient Ireland West of the River Shannon 63
- Legendary Rulers. *65*
- The Rise of Connacht's Dynastic Tribes. *66*
- The Rise of the O'Conor Dynasty *68*

CHAPTER 8   Anglo-Norman Colonization of Connacht 75
- The Founding of a Norman Colony *77*
- Decline of the O'Conor Dynasty. *78*
- "More Irish Than the Irish Themselves" *79*
- Galway: The Making of a Medieval Trading Center. *80*
- Trade and Commerce *82*
- End of Gaelic Rule *83*

CHAPTER 9   Historical Tuaths of Eastern Connacht. 87
- The Three Tuaths *88*
- Kingdom of Moylurg *90*
- The King's Cantreds *92*

CHAPTER 10   The Three Tuaths—Kinel Dofa 97
- Lifestyles, Behavior, Customs and Beliefs. *98*
- Subordinate Septs *99*
- Kilglass: From Bishopric to Parish *101*
- Changing Winds. *102*
- Anarchy Everywhere *102*
- Hanley Diaspora. *104*
- O'Donovan on Journeying Through Kilglass (1830) *104*

Chapter 11 The Three Tuaths—Corca Eachlinn 109
- *Territorial Chieftains* *110*
- *Christianity Supplants Druidism at Ona's Fort* *112*
- *Clan MacBrennan* *114*
- *MacBrennan Tribal Encounters* *115*
- *The Decline of the MacBrennans* *116*

Chapter 12 The Three Tuaths—Tir Briuin 119
- *The Early History* *119*
- *Territorial Chieftains* *120*
- *O'Monaghans Ousted by O'Beirnes* *121*
- *Decline in Status* *124*
- *Other Tir Briuin Septs* *126*

Chapter 13 Conquest and the Anglo-Irish
          Ascendancy Era 129
- *Confiscation and Plantation* *131*
- *War and More Wars* *132*
- *The Penal Laws* *134*
- *An Oppressed Peasantry* *135*
- *Emergence of a Gaelic Middle Class* *136*
- *Political and Religious Reform Progress* *137*
- *The Act of Union* *138*
- *The Emergence of Irish Nationalism* *139*
- *Demands for Self-Government* *140*
- *Landlords Under Attack* *141*
- *From Easter Rebellion to Nationhood* *142*
- *The Collapse of Ascendancy Power* *144*

Chapter 14 Ascendancy Families of Eastern Connacht 145
- *Profiles of Two Anglo-Irish Families* *148*
- *The Exodus* *150*

Chronology 153

Glossary 155
List of Illustrations 157
Bibliography. 159
About the Author. 163
Endnotes 165
Index 173

Acknowledgments

Writing this history of *Celtic Ireland West of the River Shannon* would have been most difficult, if not an unrealizable task, had it not been for the support and encouragement of many individuals.

First of all, I am indebted to my wife, Joan, who contributed many hours critiquing the manuscript: her perceptive editing smoothed out the jagged edges and her suggestions substantially added to the enhancement and clarity of the text.

An *especial muchas gracias* must go to my daughter, Edie, whose inspiration and skill on the book layout and cover design added greatly to the final touches. She also reviewed the manuscript and made important suggestions.

I would also like to mention the late Professor Brian P. Beirne, Ph.D., formerly of Simon Fraser University, Vancouver, British Columbia, Canada, who inspired me to write this book.

There were others, of course, who contributed in different ways and I would like to acknowledge their help: Patrick Brennan of Cleveland, Ohio, for sharing his research on Clan MacBrennan; Peter Hanley of McLean, Virginia, for sharing the fruits of his pursuit of the O'Hanley Clan; Jim Callery of Cloonahee, County Roscommon; Robert Gorman of Chicago, Illinois; Patrick Sheeran of Bethesda, Maryland; Damian Dodd of London, England; and the librarians and staff at Galway, Roscommon, Boyle and Sligo libraries, for bringing to my attention relevant information that I might otherwise have overlooked. To these and to anyone that I may have inadvertently omitted, I offer my sincere appreciation and thanks.

The many Irish/Celtic historians and writers I consulted will be evident throughout the book and are acknowledged in the bibliography.

In conclusion, I wish to add that I accept full responsibility for any inaccuracies that may have crept into the text, despite careful scrutiny by the editor and others.

Introduction

The dynamics of this book center on the rise to power of the early Irish dynasts, their constant warring among themselves to gain or retain power, their decline brought about by endless conflict with their kinsmen and invading Normans, and their final collapse following the confiscation of their lands by English adventurers in the seventeenth century.

Essentially, this book deals with Connacht, Ireland's western province. The earliest noted inhabitants of the area were Celtic tribes collectively called Firbolg (their Belgic-related tribes of Northern Gaul were known to Julius Caesar as the "Belgae"), a people believed to have ruled much of the province until well into the third century when they were toppled and driven into tributary status by the expansion and dominance of the Gael Ui Briuin dynasty. Thereafter, we are told, they withdrew into virtual obscurity before emerging again several centuries later.

Appropriately, the story starts out with an overview of Ireland's past: a journey back in time to prehistoric Ireland when the island was inhabited by peoples of the Mesolithic and later Neolithic Periods. These pre-Celtic peoples left us no written records, but they did leave behind extensive archaeological evidence in the form of megalithic monuments across the Irish landscape. Little survives of these early inhabitants; their beliefs, institutions and traditions have escaped us. However, we do know more about the immigrants that followed them. Known as the Celts, they dominated Ireland for more than two thousand years and, even today, some vestiges of their ways survive in the Irish-speaking households of western Ireland.

Our Celtic ancestors colonized Ireland in successive waves of migration from Britain and mainland Europe in the millennium before the

Christian era. They brought with them their culture and social structure which they superimposed on that of the island's indigenous population. It was a social structure that divided the island into many tribal kingdoms based on family ties. These were loosely joined together in aggregations of three or four into local kingdoms that, in turn, were grouped with several other kingdoms to form a provincial kingdom.

In the centuries before Christianity arrived, Celtic society was isolated and beyond the influence of the outside world. It was a society of aristocratic overlords and Iron Age warriors with a culture akin to that of Homeric Greece: kings fought kings and warriors fought each other. Its strength and stability lay in a generally diffused body of social customs and intricate laws, enforced entirely within the context of closely integrated communal units. With its system of tribal land tenure, pagan druidic beliefs, and oral tradition and language, this structure remained relatively unchanged for centuries.

The Ireland into which Christianity arrived was a country of strong religious traditions. Its people practiced an ancient pagan creed called Druidism whose chief gods were deities from a pre-Iron Age matriarchal order that personified the forces of nature. It was a religion governed by its priests (called druids) who yielded immense power in their communities. This securely established power possibly accounted for the long, drawn out struggle between Christianity and druidism that lasted for more than two centuries when the druids were finally displaced.

In many ways, druidism outlived the druids: Irish people gather together each year on the dates of ancient Celtic festivals to celebrate the rites once performed in honor of powerful pagan deities. Among the most important of these is *Samhain* (Hallowe'en). According to tradition, it was a time when the Celtic gods were particularly hostile. It was a night when the ancient gods walked among the Celtic mortals. In the more modern rendition of this pagan rite, the spirits of the Christian dead return to walk among the living.

The first and most far-reaching outside influence on Ireland's Celtic culture was Christianity in the fifth century, and its influence was powerful. It brought to Ireland a new creed and, with it, Latin culture in morality and canon law. When monastic scribes and scholars adopted the Latin alphabet in the sixth century, they set in motion a cultural transformation, the consequences of which they themselves could not have imagined. "It was the adoption of the Latin alphabet that enabled the monastic literati to record and preserve a remarkable wealth of native pre-Christian beliefs and tradition."[1]

By the seventh century, Ireland had become one of the most advanced societies in Europe. Celtic monasteries were flourishing as great centers of learning and culture, opening their doors to men of learning from at home and abroad. Over the next several centuries, the island experienced what became known as the "Golden Age of Celtic spirituality." Its great monastic schools were famed for their scholarships and artistic manuscripts. Irish monks and scribes went abroad during Europe's Dark Ages and worked tirelessly at copying the West's treasure house of literature decimated by the barbarians that had descended on Europe following the fall of the Roman Empire. According to Thomas Cahill (*How the Irish Saved Civilization*, 1995), "…single-handedly, they saved European civilization."

The introduction of Christianity into Ireland failed to make any substantial changes to the framework of Celtic society itself. While the Celtic Irish embraced Christianity, they found that its alien institutions posed problems for Gaelic society. A solution was found in reshaping those institutions along the lines of the country's own tradition of petty kings and overlords. Abbots and bishops were given a status equivalent to the tuath king, so that many abbotships and bishoprics remained within the same extended kin-group making it possible for those roles to be passed down from generation to generation.

By the time Ireland had fully assimilated into Christianity, she encountered another and very different kind of invasion. The invaders were the Vikings—originally from Norway and later from Denmark—who came first to plunder and then to settle. They began their incursions at the end of the eighth century and, by the early tenth century, had gained numerous footholds and established many permanent settlements, mostly along the eastern seaboard. They founded the kingdom of Dublin, a separate Danish territory within the Irish polity, which had numerous overseas connections. They were inevitably drawn into the shifting alliances and warfare that occupied the Gaelic lords that, in the end, may have worked to curb their expansion over the whole island. In 1014, a mighty army of Irish under King Brian Boru defeated the Vikings at Clontarf, north of Dublin, ending Viking dominance in much of Ireland. Thereafter, they settled down and became integrated into Irish society.

Elements of Norse culture endured to influence Irish culture: their artistic techniques and styles inspired Irish artisans and words from their language became imbedded in the Gaelic tongue. However, the most enduring influence of the Viking invasion on Irish life was the expansion of Irish over-lordship[2] that grew under conditions brought on by Viking attacks. Nevertheless, the growth of military over-lordships had little effect on the old tradition of political decentralized sovereignty. Sovereignty remained as fragmented as it had been before the Vikings arrived.

In the post-Viking period, cultural activity and the arts (which had experienced a setback during the Viking period) came into their own again, revealing new and exciting trends. Religious reform was undertaken and the organizational structure of the Irish Church was brought into conformity with that of the Roman model. During this time, an ambitious Connacht dynast, Turlough O'Conor, succeeded in seizing the high kingship after defeating the Mac Loughlins who had replaced the O'Neills. The O'Conors held onto power for several centuries until they brought about their self-destruction from internecine disputes and warfare with their neighbors.

After a period of relative quiet, Ireland was again invaded in the twelfth century. This time it was King Henry II and his Anglo-Norman barons from the neighboring island of Britain. The Ireland they found was still a regionalized patchwork of petty kingdoms. Henry set about consolidating this array of separate kingdoms into one kingdom, setting up a governing administration and instituting laws of a feudal society that rested on a hierarchy of authority under his kingship. It was a governing system, very different from that of the Irish, whose array of autonomous kingdoms embodied local custom rather than a unified application of rules and practices.

Despite their military prowess, Norman efforts to extend central administrative control over the whole of the island met with stubborn resistance, and the struggle between the Gaels and the Normans dragged on for centuries. In essence, it was a challenge between the aristocratic leadership of both sides—the Gaelic nobility and the Norman lords. During the three hundred years following the invasion of the Anglo-Normans, the history of Ireland was a constant seesaw of Gaelic and Norman advance and retreat. The Anglo-Norman colonization effort had little more effect than the earlier Norse invasions in altering the general state of society. Matters remained very much as they were until the time of Queen Elizabeth in the second half of the sixteenth century, at which time the old system of tribal land tenure was replaced with the English system, and English administrative law was substituted for Brehon law. But even after this time, most of the ancient native customs remained and, indeed, many still remain.

From the dawning of Celtic Ireland, the reader accompanies the early Celts on their cultural journey down the ages and into the province of Connacht. There the story centers on the early tribal communities—exploring the developing dynastic families, descendants of once "heroic" warrior societies that were given to feasting and hard drinking, eloquence, boasting, and fighting. In Connacht, some thirty petty kingdoms came to figure prominently in Irish history and legend. Among them were three known collectively as the Three Tuaths and separately as Kinel Dofa, Corca Eachlinn, and Tir-Briuin-na-Sionna.[3]

The ensuing chapters, the point of convergence of the book, take the reader to an area west of the River Shannon, the heartland of Kinel Dofa, Corca Eachlinn and Tir-Briuin-na-Sionna. The reader is presented with a microcosm of Celtic tribal life with its constant family conflicts, its chronic state of anarchy and its eventual collapse.

The final chapters cover the Anglo-Irish landed gentry period in eastern Connacht: the Gaelic families who were dispossessed and the Anglo-Irish families that replaced them. A struggle for political and religious freedom followed. It was a bloody struggle, the outcome of which saw the resurgence of Celtic culture and the triumphant return of the Irish Gaels as masters of their own destiny.

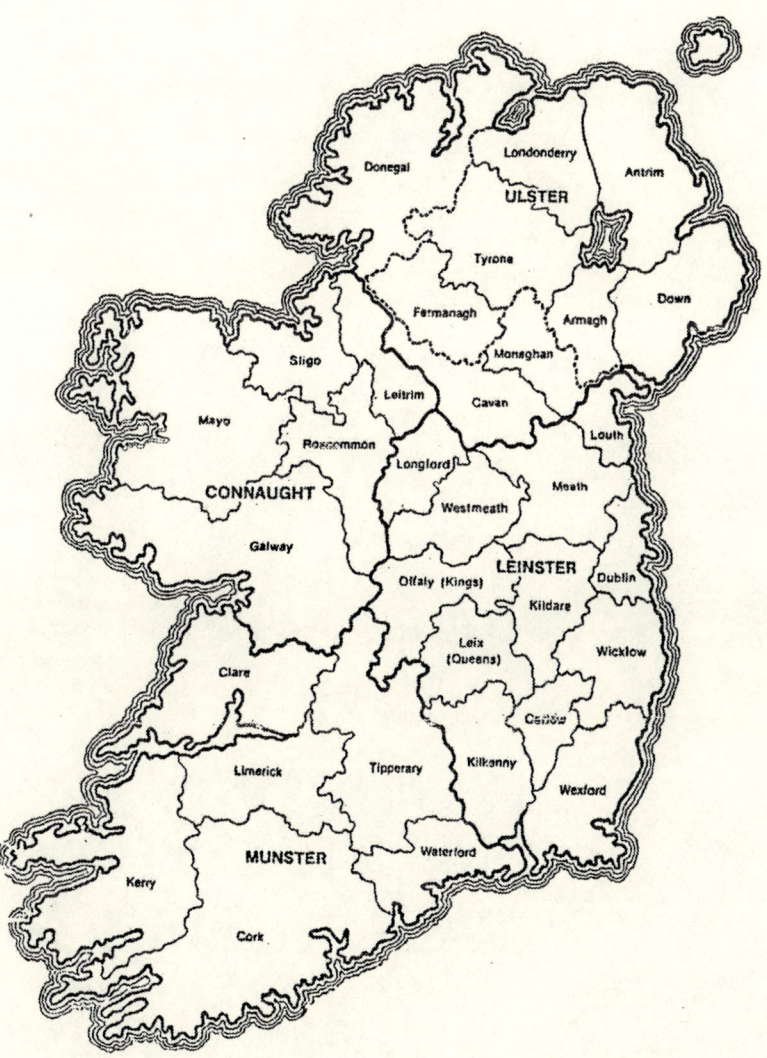

Map of Contemporary Ireland Showing Counties and Provinces

1

Beyond the Mists

o o o o o o o o o o o o o o o o o o o o o o o o o o o o o
When the Celts arrived in Ireland, the island had been inhabited for over 7,000 years. These pre-Celts have left no written records: they were literary pre-historic. But they have left extensive archaeological evidence, of which Newgrange is the most celebrated example.

—Laurence Flanagan (Ancient Ireland: Life Before the Celts)

During the Ice Age, estimated at somewhere between more than one million and most recently thirteen thousand years ago, Ireland was a part of the European land mass. At various stages in its duration, much of the country was covered by an icecap similar to what one finds in Arctic areas today. The ice cover was not continuous, however, for alternating periods of warm and cold stages caused the glaciers to retreat and expand accordingly. The question of course arises as to whether peoples may have been present in Ireland during one or another of those warmer phases when the glaciers were in retreat. To date, there is no scientific evidence of it; no Old Stone Age tools from the Paleolithic period have been unearthed, no extraordinary animal paintings such as those on cave walls in France and Spain have been discovered.

THE MESOLITHIC PERIOD (8000–4000 B.C.)

According to archaeologists, the first human visitors to Ireland arrived eight thousand years ago. They were Mesolithic people believed to have migrated across the North Channel from Scotland after the last Ice Age. The first "Irishmen" were a small dark-featured people, more than likely from the Mediterranean region, who had earlier migrated northward across Europe when the ice caps receded. We know little of them except that they lived close to lakes and rivers. They left no clues to a settled life—neither dwelling nor burial site—only some charcoal traces of their campsites and some flint tools, mostly found in the northeastern region of Ulster. Although very little is known about the Mesolithic folk who made ancient Ireland their home, it is only appropriate to begin with them.

Data extracted at sites such as Mount Sandel in County Derry and Lough Boora in County Offaly have allowed archaeologists to place the beginning of the Mesolithic period at around 7000 B.C.[4] Historian Liam de Paor writes that it is highly probable that they form the basic genetic stock of the Irish people.[5] More recently, however, genetic studies conducted by researchers from Trinity College, Dublin and Leicester University in England have shown that a high percentage of persons with Gaelic surnames extant in the province of Connacht carry a distinctive collection of genes inherited from the more recent Neolithic hunters and fishermen of pre-Celtic Ireland.[6]

THE NEOLITHIC PERIOD (4000–2000 B.C.)

Four thousand plus years later, people of the Neolithic race settled in Ireland. Their forebears had earlier transformed human survival by discovering the benefits of tilling soil and domesticating wild animals. They had long since been driven westward out of the Mideast by expanding population and arrived in Ireland around 3700 B.C., presumably by way of Gaul and Britain. They, too, were small and dark, and they also used stone tools. They were, however, more sophisticated than the Mesolithic people they displaced. They made flint arrows and stone implements for domestic need. They used stone axes to clear cuttings in the forests. They plowed, sowed and reaped, and lived in settled communities.

Data extracted from Neolithic sites such as the court tomb at Annaghmare, County Armagh and the passage tomb at Knowth, County Meath attest to the presence of a variety of domesticated animals: cows, goats and pigs. Peter Harbison, well-known authority on Irish archaeology, writes that in Connacht, particularly in north Mayo, bogs successfully covered not only court cairns, but also Neolithic field systems delineated by stone and earthen walls, which have come to light only in recent years with the extensive modern exploitation of the bogs.[7] But the most spectacular legacies of the Neolithic people of early Ireland were in the monuments of colossal stones they raised where they buried their dead and, perhaps, where they worshipped their gods.

Over the next two thousand years, the island was settled by successions of new Neolithic Stone Age invaders. Some had intensely skillful and sophisticated cultures, as can be seen by the many large stone-built chambered burial sites known as megalithic tombs dotting the countryside, the most elaborate of which is Newgrange in County Meath. Newgrange, built about 2500 B.C., around the time of the Egyptian pyramids, suggests a people with at least the sophistication of the pyramid-builders. At Carrowkeel in County Sligo, atop the Bricklieve Mountains, the ruins of another passage-tomb, less imposing than Newgrange but none the less astounding, offers the visitor a glimpse into the distant past at what living may have been like for those prehistoric settlers. Many other smaller structures, fifteen hundred identified so far, dot the Irish landscape attesting to the eccentricity of those ancient folk. Unfortunately, the Neolithic Stone Age people had no written language to pass on more information about themselves. We have no idea what language they spoke or how they worshipped their gods. The symbolism in their art is unclear to us. But their elaborate structures tell us that they were a highly skillful people.

In recent years, archeologists have built up a widely held view that suggests megalithic tombs may have been constructed by three separate invasions of peoples believed to have been from present-day France. The first Neolithic invaders were considered to have landed on the west coast of the island in what is present-day Mayo, where they constructed the first court cairns (the earliest megaliths) before moving on first into Ulster, and ultimately across the North Channel to Scotland. The second group of invaders was thought to have come from Brittany up the Irish Sea. They landed near the mouth of the River Boyne where they built the passage tombs at Newgrange, Knowth and Dowth, before heading westward via Loughcrew to County Sligo where they built Carrowmore and Carrowkeel. The great earthwork at Newgrange, situated atop a small hillock on the northern side of the River Boyne, attests to a people as advanced as the Egyptian Pyramids builders. Atop a limestone plateau overlooking breathtaking Lake Arrow at Carrowkeel, there is a burial ground which consists of a dozen or more passage tombs and linked structures, almost all in round stone mounds. On a hill some distance from Carrowmore and Carrowkeel is believed to be Queen Maeve's grave atop Knocknarea, claimed to be one of the largest passage-tombs known.

In time, the people who built Newgrange, Carrowkeel, Carrowmore, Knocknarea, and other great passage tombs were overtaken by more invaders arriving and settling intermittently between 2100–1300 B.C. Archaeological discoveries confirm a new form of burial that was introduced during this period. Single-burial graves replaced the great stone communal tombs of the Neolithic people. Skeletons recovered show a round-headed people of a racial type new to Ireland. Gracefully decorated pottery of the period shows no continuity with anything of an earlier age in Ireland. These are referred to as the Beaker people (so called for their pottery style). It is believed that their influx into Ireland, toward the end of the second millennium (1200 B.C.), signals the fading away of the traditions of megalithic burial and Bronze Age pottery forms.

About the seventh century B.C., peoples who spoke languages of the Indo-European group had established themselves all over Europe. Central and western regions of Europe were dominated by Celts, warrior chieftains belonging to one of the western branches of the Indo-Europeans. It is generally acknowledged, from several sources of evidence, that Celtic-speaking peoples were well established by this date in Gaul and Britain, and that Celtic-speakers were already settled, or settling in Ireland.

Map of Ireland from Ptolemy's *Geographia*

2

Emergence of Celtic Ireland

○ ○

The descriptions of the Celts given from about 600 B.C. onwards picture a "heroic" society of quarrelsome, boastful barbarian chiefs who were formidable in war, who drank copiously, who were head hunters, who feared nothing except "that the sky might fall."

—Liam de Poer, The Peoples of Ireland

Historians find it difficult to reconstruct the early history of Celtic Ireland. This is because the only written evidence comes from mythological tales, poems and the *Book of Invasions*, a scholarly collection of various oral traditions that was compiled in the ninth and twelfth centuries by scholarly monks. Celtic culture in Ireland, however, is generally believed to have found its roots in the last millennium B.C., during the Iron Age.

The first Celtic-speaking tribes are believed to have arrived on the island about 600 B.C. in what is referred to as the Hallstatt era. Other colonists followed them, the main thrust arriving in the later La Tene era sometime between the third and first centuries B.C. They came from neighboring Britain, Gaul and Iberia: tribes from two main stems of the Continental Celts—the Belgae[8] originating in northern Gaul and the Gael from southern Gaul and the northern seaboard of the Iberian Peninsula. They were fleeing from the Roman legions advancing across Europe at that time.

By the time Julius Caesar had completed his conquest of Celtic Europe in the first century B.C., the beginning of the end of Celtic society on the European mainland had arrived. The imperial armies of Rome next invaded Britain and again the Celts capitulated. Only in Ireland, untouched by the Romans, would Celtic culture survive and flourish, similar in many ways to what it had been in the centuries before the first Roman legions marched across the Alps to transform the face of Europe.

MEDIEVAL VERSIONS OF CELTIC INCURSIONS

Native historical renditions from medieval accounts describe four separate Celtic incursions into Ireland in pre-historic times. The Priteni were the first to colonize the island, followed by the Belgae who invaded Ireland from northern Gaul and Britain. Later, Laighin tribes from Armorica (present-day Brittany) are believed to have invaded Ireland and Britain more or less simultaneously. Lastly, the Milesians (Gaels) reached Ireland from either northern Iberia or southern Gaul. The earlier invaders are believed to have spoken a Brythonic dialect of Celtic recognized linguistically as P-Celtic. It was the language of Gaul and Britain: it survives today as Welsh, Cornish and Breton. The Gael invaders spoke the Gaelic dialect, recognized linguistically as Q-Celtic, which they brought with them from Spain. Gaelic replaced Brythonic over time as the dominant idiom of the Irish Celts and it survives today in the Irish, Scottish and Manx languages.

THE FIRST WAVE—PRITENI COLONISTS

The Priteni tribes (Ireland and Britain were known to the early Greeks as the Pritenic Islands) are believed to have arrived some time after 700 B.C. Their origin as Celts is questionable; according to some sources, they were more likely to have been the descendants of the earlier Neolithic indigenous inhabitants of the island. Probably, they were a mixture of both. Their descendants in Ireland became the Cruitin tribes, later living alongside the powerful Dal-Riada (Belgae tribes) that dominated northeastern Ulster up to the ninth century AD. The Romans, who never fully succeeded in conquering them in northern Britain, referred to them as the Picti, meaning painted people.

THE SECOND WAVE—EUERNI COLONISTS

The second wave, the Euerni, or Erainn, belonging to the Belgae people of northern Gaul, began arriving about the sixth century B.C. They called their new home Eueriio, which would later evolve through the old Irish Eriu to Eire, and from Eire to Ireland. The Erainn, more commonly referred to in contemporary references as the Firbolgs, claimed to be descendant from the god Daire through his son Lugaid, and they preserved traditions that told how their ancestor Lugaid had led an army from Britain and conquered Ireland. The significance of the legend concerning Lugaid is that it points out that the Erainn, according to their traditions, came to Ireland from Britain.[9] From Ptolemy's account of Ireland (c. 325 B.C.) there is good reason to believe that the Erainn tribes were then the most widespread and predominant on the island.[10]

After the beginning of the La Tene era, the Erainn were followed by other Belgae colonists. They contributed greatly to their adopted country with their art forms: swords, torcs and vessels very similar to those produced on the Continent. However, there is little evidence that their technological capabilities had any affect on the archaic life-style of the natives. They seem to have set up very few oppidum-like hill settlements, common in Britain and the Continent at the time. Instead, they made do with the natives' style of dwellings: rudimentary circular beehive-shaped stone houses built without mortar.

Several offshoots of the Belgae colonists can be identified: the Menappi in Wicklow, the Dal-Riada in west Antrim and the Dal-Fiatach in east Ulster. Norman Mongan maintains that many of the present nameplaces in Ireland containing syllables such as mong, muin, maine, managh, monach, manach, mannog, etc., attest to the presence of the Belgae in the area at some stage.[11]

THIRD WAVE—LAGINIAN COLONISTS

The third wave of colonization is believed to have taken place sometime about 300 B.C. They were the Laginians or, according to their own tradition, Gauls who came to Ireland from Armorica. Their name association with Laighi, the ancient name for Leinster, suggests that this was where they first settled. Another branch of the same people was the Galioin (or Gailenga) who settled in an area north of Dublin and Meath. Eventually the Galioin extended their power to northwestern Connacht and in the process forced many Belgae (Firbolg) tribes into the remoter parts of the province. One can still see, in the remoter areas of western Ireland, the remains of many great stone forts built by the Firbolgs in their defense against the Galioin.

In the *Tain Bo Cualnge* (Cattle Raid of Cooley) there is mention of three thousand Gailioin serving under Ailill and Meave in their expedition into Ulster against King Conchobar. Within a few generations, they had established themselves in northern Connacht, where in County Sligo their descendants included the O'Hara and O'Gara families. The strength of the Laginians was uppermost in south Leinster where they remained the dominant power well into historic times. They made little impact in Munster or in Ulster, suggesting that their occupation was limited to parts of present day Leinster and Connacht. Like the Belgae, the Laginian tribes were linguistically P-Celts, and had kinsmen in Britain.

The Last Wave—Milesians (Gaels)

The last major Celtic settlement in Ireland is believed to have taken place sometime between 150–50 B.C. These people have been identified as the Milesians (Sons of Mil, or Gaels) who, according to tradition, fled Roman incursions into northern Iberia and southern Gaul. These were Iron Age Celts and their dominance over the island was to last well over a thousand years. The ancient manuscript, *Leabar-Gabala*, has them landing at two locations—Kerry in the south and the Boyne estuary in the east. Those who landed through the Boyne estuary pushed the earlier Laighin settlers from their land in north Leinster and established their kingship at Tara. The southern Gaels had no fixed location in the beginning; instead they pushed inland moving from one district to another until eventually they made Cashel their headquarters.

Gael subjugation of the Belgae and Laighin occupiers of the island was, according to O'Rahilly, still incomplete as late as the beginning of the fifth century A.D.[12] The Ulaid tribe still ruled Emain and was challenging the midland Gaels for supremacy. It was only in 516 A.D. that the conquest of the midlands was finally achieved when "the Plain of Mide" was wrested from the Laighin.

Summary

Without the classical sources of information on Ireland[13] (such as that which is available from Roman and Greek sources about the Continental Celts), historians are limited to what archaeology and the vernacular literature can reveal. As always, archaeological evidence raises questions of interpretation and, as was pointed out in the previous chapter, the vernacular evidence is limited and distorted because it was written down largely by Christian scribes many centuries after the events described actually took place.

Should the medieval account of successive waves of invaders be accepted as the manner in which the Celts colonized Ireland? Historian John King is not convinced, believing that it is not supported by archaeological evidence. He goes on to suggest that the overall pattern seems to have been more complex than a single series of tribal incursions, that archaeological data shows that continental influence was trickling onto the island for hundreds of years before the main body of Celtic people began to arrive, and that the indigenous inhabitants who previously occupied the island were not eliminated, nor even conquered. King writes, "Most of the material artifacts are either from the early Hallstatt style, or in the late La Tene style (from about 250 B.C.).... There is virtually no evidence for the expected intermediate stages of late Hallstatt and early La Tene. Some evidence such as the torc found at Clonmacnoise dating from 33 B.C., appear[s] to have been imported from the continental mainland."[14]

3

The Mythical Tradition

○ ○

The Gaels tried to adjust what happened to them to fit what should have happened to them so that events originated in myth.

—Jean Markale, *The Celts*

In Ireland, mythological history is so intertwined with factual history that at times it is difficult to know where mythology ends and fact begins. This blurring of the two is part and parcel of the culture formed in part by an oral tradition that kept alive the great sagas of a heroic age (later put into writing by the Christian monks). Irish mythology describes a series of invasions that led to the establishment of Celtic Ireland. According to the mythological rendition, the invading tribes were, in succession: the Cessair, the Parthlon, the Nemed, the Fir Bolg, and the Tuatha de Danann. The story, which is told in the medieval manuscript *Leabhar Gabhala*,[15] is the embodiment of Ireland's own impressions regarding the history of her peoples.

The Cessair were a tribe of Amazons, or goddess-women, who invaded Ireland before the Great Flood. When the Flood came, the only member of the Cessair to survive was a male god, Fintan, who was Cessair's consort. He lived to Christian times, was a beholder to all the succeeding invasions, and was therefore the uppermost authority for the questions of history and tradition. Ireland had remained unpopulated for untold ages after the Flood before the Partholan took possession of the island. They fought the Fomorians (believed to have been

African pirates) who were led by the giant Balor for possession of the island. They were sheepherders who cleared the island for cultivation and introduced the peculiar practice of fosterage[16] that survived in Gaelic Ireland until recent times. We are told the Partholan all perished in a great plague. As with the Cessair, one individual survived to tell what had happened. This was Tuan Mac Starn.

Next to arrive were Nemed and his followers, who, according to Tuan, took possession of Ireland after having sailed aimlessly for eighteen months on the Caspian Sea, where many of them died of hunger before sailing west. They too were harassed by the Fomorians and were forced to pay them tribute every year at the feast of Samain (November 1). What became of them is unclear; some sources suggest that they abandoned the island and returned to their place of origin near the Caspian Sea.

Following the Nemedians, an adventurer named Senion took Ireland. From him, we are told, came the Fir Domnainn, the Fir Bolg and the Galiain tribes (offshoots of the Continental Belgae)[17] who introduced a warlike aristocracy, including weapons of metal and a system of monarchy. They did not vanish from the story like those before them; they left descendents, many of whom were enslaved by Ireland's last pre-Christian conquerors, the Milesians. Lending credence to this aspect of the legend is Ptolemy's account confirming the widespread and dominant presence of Erainn, or Belgae, tribes throughout the island as early as the sixth century B.C.[18]

Tuan continued by describing the arrival of the Tuatha de Danann and the story of the famed battle at Moytura on the Mayo-Galway border. Here the De Dananns, described as a "beautiful people descended from the goddess Dana," met and overthrew the "boorish Firbolgs" in a famed battle at southern Moytura. King Eochaid of the Firbolgs was slain and Breas (whose father happened to be a Fomorian sea-pirate) ruled the De Danann tribes for seven years. During his reign he infuriated his people by standing idly by while the Formorians constantly came ashore from their stronghold on Tory Island (off the north coast of Ireland) to pillage and ransack the countryside. He was finally overthrown and fled to the Hebrides to seek his father's help.

Breas and his father returned to Ireland with a large army only to be defeated by the De Dananns in a great battle at Northern Moytura in County Sligo. It was there that the most infamous Formorian chief of them all, Balor of the Evil Eye, who ruled Tory Island off the northwest coast, was slain by a stone from the sling of his own grandson, the great De Danann hero Lugh. After the defeat, many of the Firbolgs followed their Formorian allies to the Western Isles of Scotland, only to be oppressed by the Picts. They returned eventually to Ireland and crossing the Shannon into Connacht were received with open arms by their Firbolg kin and given lands by the celebrated Queen Maeve.

Next to take Ireland were the Gaels. They were called the Goidel people, supposedly after a remote ancestor named Goidhal Glas, who lived during the time of Moses. An ancient tale described in the *Yellow Book of Lecan* gives an intricate account of their origin and arrival in Ireland:

> "We are born of the children of Mile, of Spain. After the building of the tower of Nimrod and the confounding of languages, we went to Egypt on the invitation of the Pharaoh, king of Egypt. Nel, son of Fenius, and Goedel Glas were our chiefs when we were in the South. That is why we were called Fene, from Fenius and Gaels from Goedel Glas.... When we were in Egypt, Scota, daughter of Pharaoh the king, was given as wife to Ne, son of Fenius. That is why she is our ancestor and why we are called Scots from her. The night when the children of Israel escaped from Egypt and crossed the Red Sea dry-footed with Moses, son of Amran, the leader of God's people, and when Pharaoh and his army were drowned in the sea after keeping the Hebrews in captivity, our ancestors did not go with the Egyptians in pursuit of God's people and therefore feared Pharaoh's anger. They feared least the Egyptians reduce them to slavery as they had previously done the children of Israel. So they fled one night on Pharaoh's vessels across the shallow Red Sea to the boundless ocean around the North West of the world. They passed the Caucasian Mountains, Sythia, and India, crossed

the Caspian Sea, which lies there, crossed the Palus Maeotis and arrived in Europe; from the South East Mediterranean to the North West, right of Africa, they passed the columns of Hercules on their way to Spain and thence to this island…. It was Ith son of Breogan who saw the mountains of Irrus from the top of Breogan's tower in Spain and it was he who came to this island leaving a path for us to follow…."[19]

Another rendition of the voyage describes how they settled in Spain after much wandering in search of a new home, and there they heard stories from Phoenician traders of a green and misty isle to the north, which they took to be the Isle of Destiny foretold to them by Moses. Their leader Milesius sent his uncle, Ith, on a journey to find out more about this place. But Ith did not return. The De Danann natives, suspecting the motive for his visit, had murdered him.

Following Milesius's death, his wife (Scotia) and eight sons with their families and followers set sail for Ireland. As they neared the southwestern coast a dreadful storm overtook them, dispersing their fleet. Many in the flotilla, including five of Milesius's sons, were lost at sea. Those who survived made it ashore only to meet stubborn resistance from the De Dananns. In due course they prevailed, conquering the De Dananns in a great battle at Taillte in County Meath. The two races then agreed that the sons of Mil should keep the earth and that the De Dannans should have the underground and island regions. The De Dannans may have been banished, but their memory has endured until the present time in the guise of what the Irish country folk respectfully call "the good people."

The island was then divided among Milesius's kin as follows: Eber was given the southern half of the land; Eremon the northern half. Ith's son, Lughaid, was given the southwestern corner of Munster, and to the children of Ir went the northeastern corner of Ulster. In time a dispute arose between the followers of Eber and Eremon. Eremon was victorious and, hence, through him was established the lineage and succession to the overlordship of the Gaels in Ireland. Another version has the land divided between Eogan Mor, alias Mug Nuadat, and Conn and tells of the struggle for supremacy between the two, ending in the battle of Mag Lena.

SUMMARY

Much of what is recounted in the mythical stories of Ireland's Celtic invasions and epic past would undoubtedly fail serious critical analysis. However, combining it with that which archaeology and folklore furnish provides a key to genuine long-lost history, however distorted by the passage of time, and helps somewhat in unraveling the real story of ancient Ireland and from whence the various colonists originated. As the Romans never occupied Ireland, there are no classical sources of information, only what archaeology and vernacular literature reveals. As referenced in the previous chapter, the archaeological evidence raises questions of interpretation, and the vernacular evidence is limited and distorted because it was written down largely by Christian scribes many centuries after the events described actually took place. Nonetheless, we have to assume that the invasion myths contain at least some elements of truth, because in many instances throughout the mythical stories one can find many characteristics of early Irish Celtic society that have similarities with the better-documented Celtic societies of Britain and Gaul.

Map of Ireland c. 750 A.D. Showing Major Tribal Groups

4

Early Celtic Ireland

○ ○

With the arrival of the Celts, Ireland entered on a new phase of her history. Apart from their ruined monuments, and their blood which probably still flows in our veins, little survives of the stone age hunters and early farmers.

—T.W. Moody and F.X. Martin, *The Course of Irish History*

Celtic society in pre-Christian Ireland was isolated and beyond the influence of the civilized world in the centuries following the Gael ascendancy. Because of this it continued to function as it had in Britain and Gaul prior to Roman influence. The lifestyle was rural, strongly tribal and loosely organized into largely autonomous communities bound together by family ties, in marked contrast to the centralized and urban characteristics of Celtic societies under the sway of Roman influence. It was a heroic age that kept alive traditions that settlers had brought with them from their ancestral homelands. Kings fought kings, warriors stole wives and massacred each other. Conflict flared mainly on issues of livestock, where the rustling of cattle was a usual pretext for a call to arms. It was very much a society of tribal overlords and Iron Age warriors with a culture akin to that of Homeric Greece.

The flow of newcomers over many centuries and the inevitable assimilation has made it somewhat difficult to distinguish with certainty which tribe belonged to which people. Most pre-Gael tribes remained in place, forming the basis for the future society that would be dominated by the less numerous but more powerful Gael people. Many were reduced to subsidiary status; others, powerful enough to maintain a substantial degree of sovereignty within their well-established territories, coexisted with the new rulers.

Verse passed down from the *fili* (ancient poets) describes how tribes from the Gael, Firbolgs and Laighin peoples coexisted and intermarried. In his introduction to *Leabhar-I-Eadhra*[20] (1980), Lambert McKenna, S.J. mentions that the *fili* (who were also family historians) describe the existence of two distinct kinds of ruling families in early Ireland. To the first kind belonged the families of the conquering Gael people who had established themselves as ascendancy masters. To the second were the leading families of the pre-Gael tribes, such as the Firbolg and Laighin peoples, who, although demoted to the level of tributary folk, in many instances were allowed to carry on a certain measure of control and freedom within their communities. Their chieftains, many of whom were men of wealth and influence, were often granted noble ancestry linking them to the ruling Gael families.

But coexistence didn't necessarily mean social equality. *The Book of Genealogies* (a work of genealogical treatise), compiled in 1650 by Sligo native MacFirbis, describes the attitudes toward the Firbolgs and De Dananns. They were spoken of in unflattering terms while their Gael masters were heaped with praise. Of the Gael it was said that, "Everyone who is white of skin, brown of hair, bold, honorable, daring, prosperous, bountiful in the bestowal of property, wealth, and rings, and who is not afraid of battle or combat, they are the descendants of Milesius of Erinn." The Laighin, on the other hand, were judged as, "Everyone who is fair-haired, vengeful, large, and every plunderer; every musical person, the professors of musical and entertaining performances, who are adept in all Druidical and magical arts, they are the descendants of the De Danann." The Firbolgs received the least complimentary accolades and were said to be, "Everyone who is black-haired, who is a tattler, guileful, tale-telling, noisy, contemptible; every wretched, mean, strolling, unsteady, harsh, and inhospitable person;

every slave, every mean thief, the disturbers of every council, and every assembly, and the promoters of discord among the people, these are the descendants of the Firbolgs."

RECURRING POWER STRUGGLES

Throughout the centuries before the arrival of Christianity there were recurring power struggles between rival tribal leaders. Accounts abound telling of conflicts and battles between the north Leinster Gaels and their Laighin neighbors. An ancient poem describes Laighin tribes doing battle with the Gael rulers of the Midlands.[21] Gael dynastic rule was temporarily overthrown in the first century A.D. by non-Gael rent-paying tribes (Attacotti) led by a Carbri Cinn Cait. (The history of the Attacotti revolt is told in one of the ancient tracts called "Histories," a copy of which is in the *Book of Leinster*).[22] Tradition has it that Gael rule was restored only when the legendary Tuathal Feachtmar arrived in Ireland at the head of a foreign army. It is not certain from where he arrived; some sources suggest he returned from exile in Britain to put an end to the Attacotti rebellion. Other sources depict him as a great Gael warrior who led the ancestors of the Midland Gaels to Ireland, and overcame the non-Gael tribes (Attacotti) who had hitherto ruled the country.[23] Among the names of the pre-Christian kings of Ireland (many obviously mythical), Tuathal Techmar stands out as a great leader. He became king of Tara, imposed a permanent tribute called *bórama* on the pre-Gael tribes, and carved out a kingdom for himself in the Midlands.

Tuathal is believed to have ruled thirty years and was succeeded by Cathair Mor, who in turn was succeeded by Tuathal's grandson, Conn of the Hundred Battles (who overthrew him in a great battle in Meath).[24] Conn, a half-legendary, half-historical figure, is believed to have been king of Connacht at the time he crossed the River Shannon, settled in central Ireland, and founded the kingdom of Meath. He used this symbolic position to claim the title of king of Ireland. However,

Conn's title to the kingship of Ireland was challenged by the king of Munster, Eoghan Mor (nicknamed Mogh Nuadat meaning friend of the god Nuada). Ultimately, the two men agreed to divide the island into two spheres of influence: Leth Cuind (Conn's half) was to lie north of the line of hills between Dublin and Galway; and Leth Maga (Mogh's half) south of the line.

According to the scribes, after Conn the kingship went to his son Art, who in turn was succeeded by his son Cormac. The *Book of Ballymote* describes Cormac as a great ruler and refers to him as: "a noble, illustrious king...the world was replete with all that was good in his time: the food and the fat of the land, and the gifts of the sea were in abundance in this king's reign...."[25] The *Book of Leinster* relates how Galls, Romans, Franks, Saxons, Caledonians and other foreigners would call upon him to seek his wisdom and counsel.

Three great literary works are attributed to Cormac. The first, *Teagasc an Riogh* (Instructions of a King), is set in the form of a dialogue between him and his son Cairbre whom he was preparing to assume the kingship. The second, *The Book of Acaill*, is a code for criminal law forming part of the Irish Brehon Laws. The third, The *Psaltair of Tara*, is known only by the frequent references to it by ancient writers. Cormac's literary work would appear to confirm the tradition that there was a considerable amount of scholarly enlightenment in the Ireland of the third century A.D.

Cormac died in 267 A.D., more than a century and a half before Saint Patrick arrived. However, there is a belief that he had become a Christian before his death and, inspired by his new faith, had made a dying wish to be buried at *Ros-na-Riogh* facing the east and not with the other pagan kings at *Brugh-na-Boinne*.

During his kinship, Cormac had to contend with the autocratic Finn MacCool and his warrior militia group known as the Fianna. According to the annalists, Finn and his followers had acquired great prestige and were extending their sphere of influence over much of Ireland. Somewhat disturbed at what was developing, Cormac set about curtailing their power and prestige.

THE EMERGENCE OF THE MIDLANDS CONNACHTA DYNASTY

From Conn's descendants emerged the Connachta dynasty in the Midlands. They were an ambitious people who did not rest content with ruling only their Meath kingdom. At an early period, some pushed westward across the River Shannon to their ancestral territory, making themselves master of much of the present-day province of Connacht where they subordinated the pre-Gael tribes long established in the territory of *coiced-Ol-nEcmacht*. By the seventh century, *coiced-Ol-nEcmacht* came to be known as *coiced-Connachta* and the term Connachta, first applied to Conn's descendants in Meath, became more narrowly applied to emulate the Gael rulers of west of the Shannon.

Another of Tuathal's descendents, Niall of the Nine Hostages (c. 380–405 A.D.), expanded north into Ulster and partitioned it and his north Leinster territory among his sons, thus founding the dynastic families from which came many of the kings of Ireland. In the course of time Niall's descendents in north Leinster and their descendants in Ulster became the powerful Ui Neill dynasty. The Ui Neill continued to dominate in Ireland until the early part of the eleventh century, during which time the high kingship alternated between the southern and northern branches of the clan. In the twelfth century the O'Conors, heirs to the Ui Briuin dynasty in Connacht, assumed the high kingship and the Ui Neill finally declined in power.

SOCIAL STRUCTURE OF PRE-CHRISTIAN IRELAND

The social structure of pre-Christian Ireland was similar in many ways to that of Celtic Gaul in pre-Roman times in that the island was divided into many tribal kingdoms based on family ties. A group of families occupied a division of land called a tuath within which the members of it equally owned the land. The members of the tuath, collectively known as the *deirbhfine*, consisted of all relations in the male line of descent for five generations. Included were a man's sons, his father's brothers, his grandfather's brothers and so on, all sharing alike in the family's belongings and privileges, achievements and misfortunes. Each tuath was presided over by a chieftain elected by its freemen (who alone had that privilege) from among the many eligible members of the ruling family. The king had certain delegated powers which included leading the army in time of war and representing the tuath in time of peace, but did not include making or enforcing the laws, which belonged to an assembly of freemen. Several tuaths when allied together made up a local kingdom, which was ruled by an over-king. Local kingdoms, in turn, formed confederated alliances ruled by a provincial king.

Ancient Ireland had a well-developed and complex tribal culture consisting of a highly codified legal system that regulated relationships within and between classes, families, larger kin-groups and inhabitants of tuaths. The early Irish law tracts tell us that society within the tuath was precisely defined. Below the *ri tuaithe* (petty king) was an aristocracy composed of the noble ranks whose status was measured partly by the number of their *celi* (clients). In early Irish law, clientship was known by the Gaelic term *ceilsine*. Beneath the aristocracy were the freemen (*boaire*), persons who belonged to the franchise-holding classes whose property had a value of at least twenty-one *cumals*.[26] Also included were the learned, certain skilled craftsmen and, alone among the musician class, were the harpists. Beneath the *boaire* were the nonfree who constituted the majority of the tuath members. "Nonfree" did not mean slaves only, though there were slaves. The nonfree were those who did not have the legal rights of the freemen. They had no property or possessions; they were tenants, laborers, herdsmen, inferior craftsmen, squatters and interlopers from other territories.

Agreements were transacted collectively as all *deirbhfine* property was communal. Members were given only limited rights. Leadership of the tuath belonged to members of the great families. Noblemen of lesser rank would attain, at most, the position of retinue leader. Mastery of an art or craft enabled a man to climb the social ladder. There were no towns or centralized authorities.

The *ri tuaithe* was elected to office by a gathering of the privileged classes who, in fact, represented a minority assembly as it excluded the non-privileged members. All male descendants of a former king, extending to and including great-grandsons, were eligible to compete for the kingship spot. Primogeniture was not an advantage; superior military aptitude and leadership talent were the essential requirements. Much was expected of the person who would occupy the highest office in the tuath. By present day standards, one could reason that it was a democratic system in a way. There were flaws, nonetheless, in the modus operandi. The rule precluding primogeniture succession often meant many rival contenders for the kingship, thus producing many disgruntled contenders believing they had better qualifications and a more rightful claim.

The situation was further aggravated by a custom which prescribed that a family whose contention for the kingship had failed over four generations thereupon lost its noble status, privileges, power, prestige and its eligibility to seek election another time. Families faced with this plight stopped at nothing—murder, war or both—to avert the stigma this brought upon them. Fathers ended up fighting sons, sons fighting brothers, uncles and cousins, and so on. Family feuds were sparked off and lasted for generations. Feuds with neighboring families added to the hostilities; young warriors, determined to demonstrate their fighting qualities and suitability for kingship, led random raids into adjoining territories.

On the whole, there was little impetus toward the creation of centralized political and administrative institutions because society had little use for them. Celtic society's strength and stability lay in a generally diffused body of social customs and laws enforced entirely within the context of closely integrated neighborhood units. Political power, somewhat detached from this, was grounded not in social institutions but in tribal loyalties, in charismatic qualities of leadership, and in military skill.

Map of Ireland Showing Major Dynasties in the Ninth Century

5

Religion

I am from Ireland
From the holy land of Ireland
I ask you, lord
Come dance with me in Ireland
For Christ's own sake

—Irish Anonymous, Twelfth Century

DRUIDISM

The Irish Celts were a religious people even before they embraced Christianity in the fifth century. They practiced an ancient pagan faith, Druidism, which was akin to that practiced by the Celts elsewhere. Their chief gods were those of the Iron Age Celts, deities from a pre-Iron Age matriarchal system that personified the forces of nature. It was a religion governed by its priests who were called druids. The druids wielded enormous power over the communities where they lived. Caesar gives the first detailed account of the Celtic priestly class in Gaul: "Throughout Gaul there are only two classes of men who are of any account or importance…the druids and the knights. The druids are in charge of religion. They have control over public and private sacrifices, and give rulings on all religious questions. Large numbers of young men go to them for instruction, and they are greatly honored by the people."[27]

Caesar continues: "In most disputes, between communities or between individuals, the druids act as judges. If a crime is committed, if there is a murder, or if there is a dispute about an inheritance or a boundary, they are the ones who give a verdict and decide on the punishment or compensation appropriate in each case. Any individual or community not abiding by their verdict is banned from the sacrifices, and this is regarded among the Gauls as the most severe punishment. Those who are banned in this way are reckoned as sacrilegious criminals. Everyone shuns them; no one will go near or speak to them for fear of being contaminated in some way by contact with them. If they make any petitions there is no justice for them, and they are excluded from any position of importance."[28]

Much about Druidism and its ancient practices and rituals remains shrouded in mystery because the druids wanted it that way, and no wonder, since only they knew "the language of the gods." Ironically, our knowledge of Irish Druidism has come down to us by way of the ancient Irish monks who transcribed the oral accounts from earlier times. According to Irish tradition, the center of druidism in Ireland was in Uisneach in present-day county Meath. It was there that Mide, the first druid, lit the first fire in Ireland that blazed for seven years and could be seen across the length and breadth of the land. To the Irish, as to the Continental Druids, fire and water were the sacred elements, and early Irish law enshrines many traditions concerning the sanctity of both. The holy wells of Christian Ireland were holy wells to the druids in the pre-Christian era, and the festive bonfires lighted throughout Ireland on Midsummer Night (June 23) are of pre-Christian origin, when the people lit fires to commemorate their sun god.

Major druidical religious observances focused on the solstices, equinoxes and moon phases. For example, *Samhain*, which is the modern Irish word for November, marked the Celtic new year. It was the day on which mortals made peace with the spirits. *Imbolc*, observed on the first of February, was dedicated to the mother-goddess, Brigit, who was later Christianized into Saint Bridget. After the vernal equinox came

Beltaine, celebrated on the first of May, honoring Bel the goddess of fertility and life. *Lughnasa*, observed on the first of August was the feast of thanks to the god Lug for the harvest bounty. Druidism was essentially a nature religion. John King writes that the land with its rocks, springs, lakes and mountains was a living and sacred thing, and its gods and goddesses were manifest and omnipresent.[29] Classical texts recount how the druids attached particular importance to the belief that the soul does not perish but passes after death from one body to another.

Druidism did not end abruptly with the arrival of Christianity to Ireland. Contrary to popular belief, Saint Patrick's progress in converting the Irish to the new faith wasn't universal. In his *Confessions*, Patrick leaves little doubt as to the difficulties he encountered: his imprisonment and his constant fear for his life as he labored to convert the pagan Irish. It is thought that as late as the sixth century Irish society was still mainly pagan in its legal and administrative functions, and that it was into the seventh century, or beyond, before the Christian clergy were fully accepted into the privileged rank of *fili*, previously the domain of the druids. This has given rise to the view that Druidism and Christianity endured side-by-side long after Saint Patrick's time.

CHRISTIANITY

Christianity, arriving in the fifth century A.D., was the first major outside influence on Ireland's Celtic culture. The first mission by Saint Palladius was less than successful in converting the polytheistic druids and their followers. Saint Patrick, arriving in 432 A.D., was more successful in persuading the Irish Celts to embrace the new Faith. It is sometimes assumed that everything altered radically when the Christian religion was introduced, but this was not the case. Many of the founding saints of Celtic Christianity were people of high social standing, the very people who, in earlier generations, would have become druids. According to the early texts, traditional tribal territories were left intact, and so were the ancient, traditional sacred places, the hallowed hereditary preserves of the families that possessed them. Ironically, it was not Celtic or even Roman Catholic Christianity that led eventually to the indiscriminate effacing of Celtic sacred sites; it was the Reformation. When the Catholic Church was suppressed in Britain and Ireland, sacred places were banned for being alleged objects of superstition.

A Scottish Parliamentary Act of 1581 sums up the attitude of the Puritans: "The Dregs of Idolatry yet remain in divers Parts of the Realm by using Pilgrimage to some Chapels, Wells, Crosses, and such other Monuments of Idolatry, as also by observing the Festal days of the Saints sometime Named their Patrons in setting forth of Bon-Fires, singing of Carols within and about Kirks at certain Seasons of the Year."[30]

Druidism was hereditary and it was only natural that the holy men who became Christians continued their hereditary rights over the places of their ancestral religion. These hallowed sites gradually acquired the basic nature of the newer creed, while retaining the essence of the older faith. In due course, a "dual faith" came into being in which an official Christian liturgy was augmented by vernacular Pagan customs and usage. Localized legends of the old gods and heroes were seen and understood as topics in the lives of the Christian saints. The worship of founder-clerics, universally called saints (although never canonized by the Roman Church), was added to traditional ancestor- and hero-worship.[31]

While the teachings of the Christian Church had a powerful influence on Gael culture, it failed to make any substantial transformation to the framework of Celtic society itself. Instead, it adapted itself to fit existing Celtic political institutions. Saint Patrick is generally thought to have organized his church in accordance with the Continental model of parishes assembled into dioceses presided over by bishops. Within a generation of his death, the Irish began embracing monasticism in a big way and the Irish church became organized on very different lines, with monasteries rather than parishes as the key units. The consequence was that abbots generally had more power and influence than bishops.

New monasteries replaced many of the older Patrician institutions as the important centers of religion and learning, and Ireland became unique in western Christendom in having its most important churches ruled by a monastic hierarchy, most of whom were not bishops. Tómas Ó'Fiaich writes that even in Armagh, the church (which was looked upon in a special way as Patrick's own) soon accommodated itself to the new system. Patrick's immediate successors were first bishops, then abbots who were bishops. By the eighth century, the abbot was no longer a bishop but had, as a subordinate member of his community, a bishop for the administration of those sacraments for which Episcopal orders were necessary.[32]

Theories abound as to how this monastic takeover in Ireland came about. Historian Paul Johnson suggests that trading links between Ireland and the Loire Valley exposed the Irish to the monastic movement flourishing in Gaul at the time.[33] Other writers believe it all began with the arrival in Ireland of monks fleeing the vast hordes of vandals spreading throughout Gaul following the collapse of Roman rule. They brought with them the rules of monasticism pioneered by Saint Martin of Tours. Whatever the reason, by the end of the sixth century monasticism had become Ireland's dominant religious form with several hundred monasteries operating throughout the country. Territorial bishoprics gave way to monastic houses whose members owed allegiance to an institution, the head of which was an abbot. Irish monasticism became wholly integrated with local society. Abbots were nearly always members of the ruling clan or tribal family; and monastic holdings covered huge areas of land.

Monasteries were not religious institutions in the restricted sense; they existed and flourished as great centers of learning and culture, opening their doors to scholars of all kinds. They helped transform rural Irish society by providing the country with the closest thing to town-like communities. The larger monasteries, for example Cloonmacnoise and Armagh, provided commercial and administrative networks and were centers of trade and law, as well as learning.

Culturally speaking, Ireland was from the sixth century onward one of the most advanced societies in Europe. Its monks went abroad and became celebrated for spreading learning throughout Britain and Europe. They achieved great missionary success wherever they went, whether it was at Iona, Lindisfarne, Luxeuil, Richenau, or elsewhere throughout Europe. Their esteem as religious pathfinders and scholars became well established during the Dark Ages of Europe. Paul Johnson writes of the Irish monks: "They were enormously learned in the scriptures, and wonderfully gifted in the arts. They combined exquisite Latin scholarship with a native cultural tradition which went back to the La Tene civilization of the first century...."[34] At a time when barbarians were descending upon European cities plundering artifacts and burning books, Irish monks and scribes were painstakingly copying the classics of Latin and Greek literature.

The Celtic monks were great sailors and the early texts recount many of their voyages beyond the shores of Ireland. The semi-mythical Brendan the Navigator, who founded the monastery of Clonfert in Galway, and who died about 580 A.D., was reputed to have undertaken a remarkable series of voyages to mysterious lands. One in particular is full of similar astounding encounters to that of the Voyage of Maelduin found in both the *Lebor na hUidre* and in the *Yellow Book of Lecan*, but with a Christian twist: a whale appears on Easter Day so that Brendan and his followers can climb on its back to hold their Easter service; one of the companions dies after seeing the pain of Hell, but Brendan restores him to life; and so on.[35]

Saint Columba took his mission from Ulster to the Western Isles of Scotland, where he founded a monastery at Iona. From there, during the course of a century, Irish monks moved in a great arc around the north-western fringes of the British Isles, reaching the English kingdom of Northumbria where Saint Aidan established a sister-house at Lindisfarne in 634 A.D.

Irish monks also traveled eastward to the Continent where one of the most remarkable expeditions of an Irish monk was that of Saint Columbanus, born c. 540 A.D. He was a tribal leader who was also head of a family monastery. He was a learned man who studied Latin and Greek and read Virgil, Pliny, Horace, Ovid and the writings of the early Fathers of the Church. Saint Columbanus left Ireland for Gaul with a shipload of monks in 575 A.D. There he began spreading his own austere brand of monastic Christianity with zealous passion. His was one of the most remarkable missionary expeditions in history. By the time he died in 615 A.D., he and his followers had spread Christianity across much of France, Italy and Switzerland and had founded more than forty monasteries.

The contribution of men such as Saint Columbanus and Saint Columba is fittingly told in Thomas Cahill's *How the Irish Saved Civilization* (1995): "From the fall of Rome to the rise of Charlemagne—the 'dark ages'—learning, scholarship, and culture disappeared from the European continent. The great heritage of western civilization—from the Greek and Roman classics to Jewish and Christian works—would have been utterly lost were it not for the holy men and women of unconquered Ireland."

But Columbanus's success, and that of other Irish monks in Europe over time, brought the character of Celtic monasticism to the attention of Church authorities who envisioned it as a threat to the Church's oldest and centralized institution, the episcopate. It was only a matter of time before Rome stepped in to contain and regulate the Celtic monastic movement that had spread throughout Europe. After the collapse of Emperor Justinian's restored empire, Pope Gregory approved the Benedictine rule[36] as the norm for monasticism in the West.

THE RISE OF THE ASCETIC *CELI DE*

Back in Ireland, as monastic communities expanded under resourceful administrators into important centers of commerce, culture and wealth, they were also becoming more secular, politically powerful and spiritually depraved. This worldliness and laxity led to a powerful and puritanical movement creeping into the Irish Church in the eighth century. It was known as the *Celi De*,[37] or Culdees, and it continued through the ninth century. In its religious renewal, the *Celi De* reached back to the early Celtic Church embracing its philosophy and ascetic practices.

One of the leaders was Mael Ruain who founded his monastery at Tallaght southwest of present-day Dublin. He adopted the rule of the Order of Canons founded on the Continent some twenty-five years earlier. It was a rule for an intermediate class of clergy between cloistered monks and secular priests who, though not fettered by monastic vows, wished to live in common within the virtuous confines of severe discipline.

The Rule of the *Celi De* was a harshly restrictive regime. Discipline was severe. In reaction to the lax monastic morals of his day, Mael Ruain decreed absolute chastity for all who had taken vows. Women were shunned. The sanctity of Sunday was absolute. Tallagh and its sister houses elsewhere were established along the lines of the early monasteries, collecting tithes from the surrounding farmers and each following its own rule under the absolute direction of its abbot. In time, the *Celi De* enmeshed themselves in secular affairs, even to the extent of taking military action. Feidlimid, king of Cashel in the mid-ninth century, besides being one of Ireland's foremost kings, was a bishop and a reformer who used the *Celi De* sect to enforce his convictions on monasteries he believed were not in conformity with the strict rules of *Celi De*. Enraged when Clonmacnoise refused to accept his candidate for abbot, he laid siege to the monastery, killing many of its inhabitants.

The excesses of Feidlimid and those like him destroyed whatever basis of credulity they had, and in a matter of time the movement lost its support. The constitutional structure of the Irish Church remained unchanged at least for the time being: responsible to no central authority, with each community self-ruling and subject only to the tenets and temperament of its leader.

Far ahead of Europe as she was in intellectual attainment, Ireland's political organization remained that of a primitive society, its structure based on the clan unit. Untouched by centuries of foreign invasion, she had developed a remarkable sense of racial and cultural unity, but there was no nationality concept. There was no central authority to enforce the law. All that was about to change by a new invasion. At the close of the eighth century, shiploads of Scandinavian seafarers appeared out of the blue, at first to raid and plunder monasteries of their wealth and then to establish trading communities.

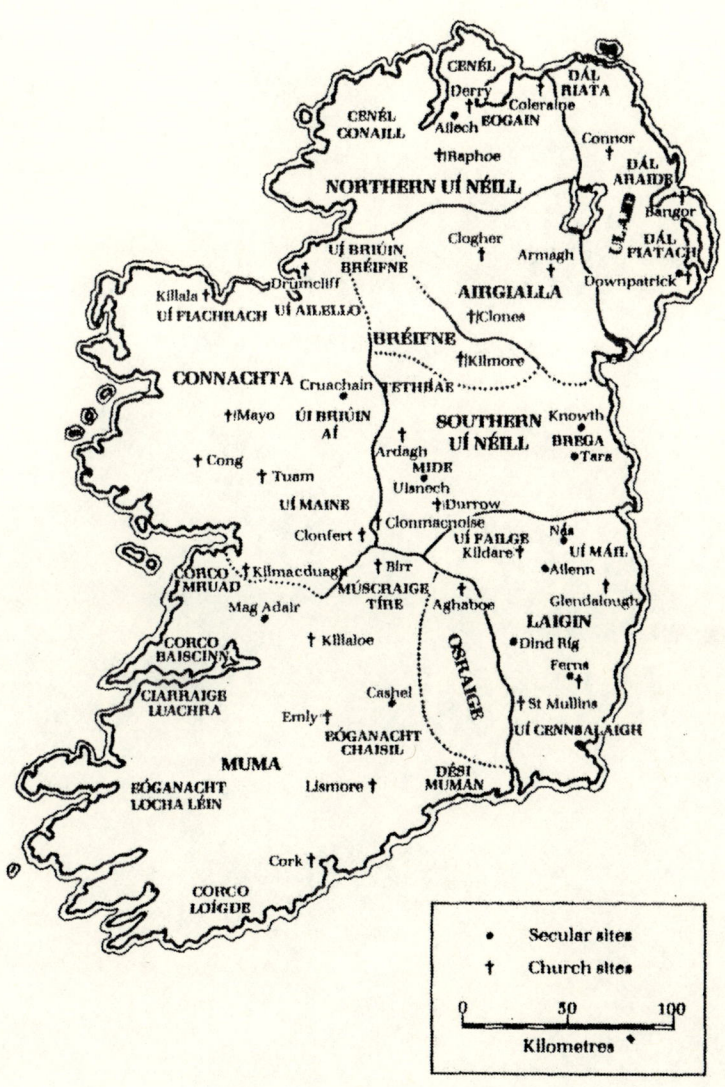

Map of Early Historic Ireland

6

Medieval Ireland

o o o o o o o o o o o o o o o o o o o o o o o o o o o o o

Oh, Where, Kincora! Is Brian the Great?
And where is the beauty that once was thine?
Oh, where are the princes and nobles that Sate
At the feast in thy halls, and drank the red wine?
Where, oh, Kincora?

—*Translated by James Clarence Mangan*
From Kincora (Eleventh Century)

VIKING INVASION

Ireland had been a Christian country for most of four centuries when the Vikings raided the island at the end of the eighth century. The first signal that the raiders from the north had arrived came in 795 A.D. when a Viking ship landed on Rechru Island (now Lambay off Howth). They sacked and burned Rechru, along with some other small islands north of Dublin. Two years earlier, the first Vikings had ventured out of the valleys and fjords of western Norway in their highly maneuverable longboats and raided the northwest coast of England, destroying the monastery at Lindisfarne. From there they had sailed north to the islands of Shetland and Orkney, and later around the tip of Scotland to the Atlantic coast to Iona, which they raided shortly before they landed at Rechru.[38]

For Ireland, the invasion of Norsemen marked the beginning of two centuries of raiding and plunder. At first, the terrorized Irish looked upon the visits as an inescapable curse from God. "Deliver us O Lord from the wrath of the Vikings," became a monk's ninth century prayer. The chroniclers of the period repeatedly accused the Vikings of widespread plundering and destruction, a view that is magnified in the twelfth century saga of *The Wars of the Gaedhil and the Gaill*: "They ravaged her kingdoms and her privileged churches and her sacred places, and they rent her shrines and her reliquaries and her books...they killed the kings and chieftains, the royal heirs and royal princes of Ireland...."[39]

However, contemporary historians caution that much of what was then written about the scale of Viking raids and extent of their settlements was greatly overstated. The chroniclers were the monks whose monasteries, rich in treasures of gold and silver, were particularly vulnerable to the reconnoitering parties. At first, there was little organized resistance from the Irish mainly because in ninth-century Ireland there was no one leader responsible for the defense of the island as a whole. As it had been for centuries, it was a land of many tribal kingdoms with a traditional division of two halves: Conn's half ruled by the O'Neills of Tara and Moga's half ruled by the Eoganachta of Cashel.

After 830 A.D., the Viking nuisance turned into a full-fledged war. Increasing numbers of attackers thrust their way inland, plundering monasteries far from the sea and taking prisoners for ransom. The incursions were also becoming more organized and on a larger scale; fleets rather than single ships or small groups of ships began appearing in Irish waters in 837 A.D. With the arrival of these fleets, the Vikings changed their strategy. They began to establish permanent settlements, building fortified colonies, consolidating and extending their power with strongholds that would later become Dublin, Cork, Limerick, Wexford and Waterford.

A Norseman named Olaf founded the kingdom of Dublin, a separate small territory within the Irish polity, but with extensive overseas connections. Another Norseman named Turgeis "assumed the sovereignty of all foreigners in Ireland." In 845 A.D., according to the annalists, Turgeis met his downfall in a battle against King Malachy of Meath, where he was taken prisoner and drowned in Loch Owel. After his death we read that the tide of victory turned for a while in favor of the Gaels.

From 850 A.D. onward, the Norse were drawn more and more into Irish affairs, playing a part in the baffling and shifting alliances of the world of the Gaels: battles within kingdoms and battles between kingdoms. These circumstances led to the growth of alliances, which in turn expanded the role of the Gael overlords. From the late ninth century onward, the O'Neill overlords in the northern half of the island had taken up an active anti-Viking policy. Nonetheless, new large-scale Viking attacks became a formidable menace again, and they gained possession of numerous areas of the island during the first part of the tenth century. Whereas the original Vikings were from Norway, these attackers were from Denmark led by Tomrair who, according to some sources, was the son of the king of Denmark. Towards the middle of the century, however, victory seemed to be on the side of the Gaels again. They had acquired from their foe the art of building naval vessels and the use of naval tactics, which they began to use effectively in their naval battles on the Shannon and inland waterways.

History records that by the second half of the tenth century, the character of the Scandinavian colonists in Ireland had changed considerably from what it had been one hundred years earlier.[40] Many Vikings had become Christian and there was much inter-marriage with the native Gael. The *Annals* describe how Olaf, son of Sitric, ruler of Dublin, died in penance at Iona in 980 A.D. Dublin had become a great trading center, as had other Viking settlements. Viking colonies were co-existing alongside Irish tuaths.

However, it was not until the end of the tenth century that the final curbing of the Norse expansion took place. It came about when an east Clare family of the Dal Cais clan rose to power by capturing the kingship of Munster from the Eoghanacht dynasty. Its leader, King Brian Boru, aggressively pursued the Vikings and within a few years brought first Limerick, then all of Munster, under his control. He went on to capture the high-kingship of Ireland from the O'Neills, and in 1014 led an army that routed the Vikings at the Battle of Clontarf, ending Viking dominance in much of Ireland. After Clontarf, the Vikings settled down and became integrated into Irish society. There is mention in some chronicles that a final attempt to conquer the island was made in 1098 when Norwegian king Mangus Barelegs (so named because he dressed like the Irish) arrived in Ireland at the head of a powerful force. Having already conquered the Hebrides and the Isle of Man, he was making a final attempt at conquering Ireland. Little is known of his incursion except that he was killed in battle somewhere in Ulster in the year 1103.[41]

The Norse left many permanent marks on Ireland. Their techniques and styles influenced Irish artists. Words from their language appear in many of Ireland's place names such as Waterford, Wexford, Leixip and Longford, to name a few. Historians suggest the expansion of Irish over-lordship was perhaps the most enduring influence of the Vikings on Irish life. In some ways changes had been slowly emerging before the Vikings arrived, but expanded rapidly under conditions brought on by Viking attacks. It was a matter of circumstances necessitating events: petty kings, lacking in resources to ward off Viking attacks, looked to their overlords who could provide larger and better equipped armies. However, the growth of military over-lordships had little affect on the old tradition of political decentralized sovereignty. It was too ingrained in the social fabric of Gaelic society to allow for any movement towards centralized authority rule. Sovereignty remained fragmented, and the traditions and institutions of Gaelic Ireland continued much as they had before the Vikings arrived.

POST-VIKING PERIOD

The eleventh and twelfth centuries were witness to a renaissance in Ireland. Cultural activity and the arts, which had experienced a setback from the Viking raids, came into their own again revealing new and exciting trends. Religious reform within the Irish Church, badly needed after a period during which many abuses had crept in, was undertaken and the organizational structure was brought into conformity with that of the Continental model. In the political sphere, the accession of Brian Boru to the high-kingship had established a departure from past custom. In many ways it set the course for a strong central monarchy, but in the century or so following the Battle of Clontarf (1014) there was considerable ongoing strife among the various Gael dynastic families. Despite Brian's efforts, there was little movement towards the creation of centralized political institutions. Celtic society derived its coherence from social customs and laws enforced entirely within the context of closely integrated communal units; political power was grounded not in social institutions but in tribal loyalties, charismatic qualities of leadership and military skill.

For the first one hundred years after the Battle of Clontarf, the Munster descendents of Brian managed to maintain their claim to supremacy. Then in the twelfth century, the northern O'Neills asserted themselves again for two short periods. The greatest challenge to their supremacy came from the ambitious Connacht dynast, Turlough O'Conor, a powerful competitor. He became the most widely acclaimed king after defeating the northern dynast, Mac Lochlainn, who had replaced the O'Neills. But the rivalry would continue for another generation with Mac Lochlainn challenging O'Conor every step of the way. When Turlough died in 1156, Malachy Mac Lochlainn, with the aid of the Leinster king Dermot MacMurrough, succeeded in grabbing the high-kingship. The O'Conors recaptured it again when Turlough's son Rory defeated Mac Lochlainn in a bloody clash in 1166.

Following his success, Rory and his client-ally O'Rourke moved against MacMurrough, driving him out of his kingdom of Leinster on the pretext he had abducted O'Rourke's wife. MacMurrough, determined to recapture his territory and restore his fortunes, sought help from neighboring England. He crossed over to Bristol in 1166 and managed to recruit parties of adventurous Normans willing to serve in return for land and position in Ireland. With the backing of the Normans, he recaptured control of Leinster.

O'Conor could not afford to overlook this serious reversal of affairs, so he assembled an army and marched against MacMurrough. Apparently, without engaging in battle, both men entered into a treaty leaving the kingdom of Leinster to MacMurrough. In return, MacMurrough acknowledged O'Conor as high king, and promised he would remove all foreign mercenaries in his service as soon as peace was restored in his kingdom. Whether or not MacMurrough really intended to observe this treaty with O'Conor is difficult to say. In any case, the adventurous Norman lords kept coming. In the process, they established a foothold on the island, and thus began the Anglo-Norman colonization of Ireland: first Maurice FitzGerald at the head of an army, followed by the Earl of Pembroke (better known as Strongbow) and a host of others. With the death of Rory in 1198, the O'Conor dynastic sovereignty in Ireland began a protracted decline.

Anglo-Norman Invasion

The Normans invaded Ireland near the end of the twelfth century, leading to centuries of armed conflict. The Irish invasion, an extension of the invasion of England and Wales a century before, began as an action of Norman lords who were acting more or less independently of the crown. Once successful, their invasions were embraced by their king, Henry II, who arrived on October 17, 1171 at the head of a large fleet. He set up court in Dublin, proclaiming himself as "Lord of Ireland." Ireland was one more sovereign claim in King Henry's array of dominions that included England and Wales, and Normandy, Anjuv, Maine, Poitou and Aquitaine as well. Henry, a Frenchman born in Normandy, was raised in France and spoke only Norman French. He had the blessing of the papacy for his expedition into Ireland.[42] Some fifteen years earlier, Pope Adrian IV, the only Englishman ever to sit on the papal throne, issued a Bull (Laudabiliter) empowering Henry to enter Ireland for the purpose of reforming the nonconformist religious practices of the island.

The Ireland to which King Henry and his lords arrived was, as it had been for centuries, a regionalized patchwork of petty kingdoms. Rory O'Connor, the high king, lacked specific authority to enforce law and order. There was no concept of national community, and societal unity existed only as far as a common language and cultural tradition were concerned. There were countless raids, counter-raids and acts of bravery and brutality between belligerent overlords.

Henry hoped to consolidate this array of separate kingdoms into one kingdom under his kingship. He set up a governing administration under a chief governor and a council of ecclesiastics and laymen. In essence, it was a colonial administration serving only the jurisdiction of the Norman settlers. It created a separate sphere of influence from that of Gaelic Ireland to which only the colonists belonged. Its law was that of a feudal society which rested on a hierarchy of authority under a kingship. The Norman customs and institutions were at first strange to the Irish whose array of autonomous kingdoms embodied local custom rather than a unified application of rules and practices.

Despite their military prowess, Norman efforts to extend centralized administrative control over the whole of the island met with stiff resistance from King Rory O'Conor and his allies. Armed conflict lasted for a few years until O'Conor, sensing that military victory was escaping him, agreed to make peace. The Norman warriors, with their superior weapons and skilled archers clad in iron helmets and suits of armor, contrasted sharply with the Irish soldier carrying his axe and short sword, clad only in a linen tunic. The result was the Treaty of Windsor

(1175) that ceded to Rory the kingship of the province of Connacht and the high-kingship of the areas of the country not under Norman influence, for which he agreed to pay Henry an annual tribute and act as a peacekeeper. In return, Henry promised to discontinue granting Irish land to his Norman lords. However, the Treaty of Windsor turned out to be nothing more than a meaningless concordant: Henry failed to keep his promise and continued to grant Irish land to his lords. Rory, on the other hand, did not have the military support from the provincial leaders to engage as a peacekeeper.

The struggle between the Gaels and the Normans continued, but it was in essence a challenge between the aristocratic leadership of both sides—the Gaelic nobility and the Norman lords. Whenever the Normans displaced a Gaelic overlord, they made little effort to displace the common folk whose duties were to herd the livestock and till the soil. Accordingly, much of the countryside remained traditionally Gaelic and relatively untouched by Norman laws and customs.

STRUCTURE OF NORMAN-IRISH SOCIETY

Henry II set in motion a system of governing that eventually lead to centralized government in Ireland. Its basis was the occupation of the land set forth in accordance with the design of Norman feudalism. As in England, the king would enjoy the right of prerogative wardship: that is, he had the wardship of all the lands as a tenant-in-chief, even though some were the domain of other lords. Government, in its early stages the direct and personal affair of the king, was modeled on that of England, evolving along the same lines throughout the Middle Ages and beyond. Since the king did not reside in Ireland, he appointed a deputy to represent him there. At one and the same time, this deputy was military chief, civil administrator and preeminent justice, subject of course to the king's override.[43]

In his governing role, the Anglo-Norman king had two advantages denied to his Irish counterpart: firstly, in the centralized monarchical authority and secondly, in the active support of an ecclesiastical hierarchy. An Anglo-Norman king had no challengers in the application of law to social disputes as had an Irish king who had the professional law-minders (Brehons) to contend with. As Celtic law was the bedrock of a society that knew no other form of security, the steadfastness of law became an article of faith among its exponents. The English Church, Catholic at the time, helped the Anglo-Norman monarchy in several ways: it tended to favor a strong kingship as the guarantee of law and order; it tended to favor a unified government because it facilitated church government; it cut across and tended to diminish political exclusiveness; and its ceremony of coronation helped to minimize the dangers of competing contenders for power.[44]

By contrast, the Irish church had been tribalized and jurisdictional authority resided not with the bishop (who possessed only the power to bless and consecrate), but in the abbots (frequently hereditary) of the tribal monasteries. Irish communities were in practice ruled by a kind of triarchy: king, abbot and brehons. A king had to contend not only with rivals but also with a fundamental social conservatism defended by deeply entrenched vested interests. The bishops, seeking a European-type monarchy as the better prospect for Continental-style bishoprics, lost out to the traditionalists among whom in the twelfth century the rulers of Connacht were the most apparent.[45] But the winds of change were beginning to blow, however gently at first, gradually altering the institutions of the Church and the manner by which they were governed.

The Medieval Church in Ireland

Between the introduction of Christianity in the fifth century and the end of the Viking wars in the eleventh century, the Church in Ireland, for the most part, administered to the spiritual needs of the Irish people with little outside intervention. Though in communion with Rome, it was to a large degree self-governing and self-renewing.[46] Over the centuries, its organization and practices had developed uniquely dissimilar to the Church elsewhere in western Europe. Hereditary lay administrators controlled monasteries and church property. Its organization was monastic rather than diocesan, a feature that resulted in a lack of priests engaged in pastoral work. Following the Viking wars and subsequent upheavals, there was spiritual and moral laxity. Deeds of violence were frequent. The sacraments were neglected and the marriage laws of the Church were disregarded. Practices such as incestuous marriages within near degrees of kindred and the reluctance to pay tithes were among the abuses contrary to Church law. There was a great need for spiritual renewal and reform of the Church itself.[47]

Reform was inevitable if Christianity was to survive in the land of "saints and scholars." Influenced by Church reform already taking place on the Continent, and more significantly the changes which had occurred at home in the Norse ruled towns, change had begun. Earlier, the christianized Norsemen of Dublin and other settled towns had aligned themselves with Canterbury for Episcopal consecration, and this had laid the foundation enabling the later Norman colony to bring the island into closer contact with the papacy than ever before. However, reform and reorganization was to remain purely theoretical for several decades because the existing establishment involved innumerable vested interests. There were some survivals from the older system: in Ulster and Connacht there were still *coarbs*[48] and *erenachs*[49], but they were no longer important.[50]

By the early thirteenth century, a degree of progress had been achieved. The country was divided into archbishoprics at Armagh, Dublin, Cashel and Tuam, and in each were established bishoprics. The arrival of the friars (especially the Dominicans and Franciscans from abroad) brought a whole new world of enlightenment to the country. It was a time of prosperity made possible by the lavish endowment of the Church with land, and the building of abbeys and friaries that sprang up everywhere. Many ruins of these once magnificent buildings can still be seen in the Irish countryside.[51]

CLIMATIC CHANGES AND CALAMITIES

Enter the fourteenth century and we find a chain of calamities as recorded in the *Annals of Connacht*. There were various human disease epidemics, great cattle plagues and nearly all the sheep died in one year. There were five years when extremes of snow, cold or gales destroyed cattle, produce and buildings, sometimes people as well. Shortages were widespread and in one year there was a great famine. Severe frost lasted from November 1434 to February 1435. This was the period known as the Little Ice Age. It began in the 1300s and was at its peek in the 1500s to 1700s. The climate was more severe than it had been for thousands of years. The long, wet winters and cool summers shortened the growing season by an average of a month. Wolves roamed the countryside and many people were devoured.

More critical to a population that lived off the land were the weather extremes that destroyed food sources and produced food shortages and famines, which increased the susceptibility of the people to epidemics of the diseases that were already indicatory by squalid conditions. Whether or not this had a restraining influence upon the combative kings and chieftains is speculative at best. But the clans appear to have been relatively subdued from the 1400s onward; possibly because they did not have the resources or the energies to initiate successful military campaigns.

Especially devastating were the epidemics of the Black Death in 1348 and 1349. The great plague swept through Europe and in the process killed more than one-third of the population. In Ireland, according to accounts, cities such as Dublin, Cork and Drogheda were almost completely depopulated within a few weeks. The ravages of the plague were presumably greatest in the towns where conditions were most favorable for the spread of infection. It is believed to have also been widespread in the countryside, having reached beyond the River Shannon by 1349, where the *Annals* refer to it in Moylurg in north Roscommon. Many believed that the plague was going to sweep everyone away and bring the world to an end. Populations elsewhere in Europe took five or six generations to recover, and there is no reason to believe it was any different in Ireland.[52]

COLONIAL RETROGRESSION SETS IN

In the three hundred years following the invasion of the Anglo-Normans, the history of Ireland was a kaleidoscope of Gaelic and Norman advance and retreat. The twelfth century Norman colonization, which began so promisingly under Henry II and expanded so vigorously for a while under his successor King John, began a steady decline near the end of the thirteenth century. The result was a remarkable Gaelic cultural revival that imperiled colonial settlements everywhere. The recovery of lost territories was remarkable as Gaels mounted attacks on Norman strongholds.

The battle of Callann in 1261, one of the great Gael victories, virtually secured the future independence of the great lordship over which the MacCarthys ruled for the remainder of the Middle Ages. Around the same time, the O'Donnells of Donegal consolidated their sovereignty at the battle of Credran where they halted Anglo-Norman expansion into the northwest. Several unsuccessful attempts were made at reviving the old high kingship, including an offer to King Haakon of Norway who died before he could land in Ireland. From the Western Isles of Scotland came heavy-armed, battle-axe-bearing mercenaries, better known as galloglasses, in support of the Gaelic chieftains in their fight to overcome the colonists. Edward Bruce, brother of King Robert of Scotland, came at the head of a large fighting force and after a succession of victorious battles was crowned high king in 1315. But his reign was short lived when he was killed at the battle of Faughart in 1318.

At the same time, powerful Anglo-Norman families such as the Earls of Desmond, Osmonde and Kildare were identifying more and more with the Gaelic culture. Described as "more Irish than the Irish themselves," they began to regard Ireland as their country and were challenging the authority of England. Alarmed and determined to curb the "decay of the colony and keep it from being completely submerged in Gaelic ways," the Statutes of Kilkenny, passed in 1366, banned intermarriage, concubinage and fosterage of children between the colonists and the native Gael. Anglo-Normans could no longer take Irish names or use the Irish language and no Gael could be appointed to an ecclesiastical office in Anglo-Norman areas of the island. Nevertheless, by the end of the century, the Kilkenny statutes had started to unravel and the Dublin administration, under the stewardship of the Gaelicized Fitzgerald earls, had gained a measurable degree of quasi-independence. It appears that Connacht was functionally outside the sphere of the Dublin government.

A culture of disorder and lawlessness was developing throughout the island among the Gaelic chieftains, which included certain sections of the Anglo-Norman society. England began to worry that Ireland would become an independent kingdom, but her wars with France and Scotland at the time made it increasingly difficult to find enough money to fight in Ireland as well. Finally, peace with France and a truce with Scotland at the end of the fourteenth century gave King Richard II the break needed to intervene in Irish affairs. In the autumn of 1394, he came at the head of a large army and waged a successful war, forcing the powerful King Art MacMurrough of Leinster to come to terms with him. Soon all the Gaelic leaders submitted to Richard and it looked as if the Gaelic expansion had been checked at last.

Within a few months of his returning to England, the war had broken out again forcing an angry Richard to return in 1399. While waging war in Leinster against McMurrough, word reached Richard that his enemy, Henry of Lancaster, had seized the English throne. He returned to England immediately, leaving the Irish problem unresolved. Never again in the Middle Ages did an English king visit Ireland. The colony continued to shrink as the Gaelic area continued to expand. The new Lancastrian dynasty in England, beset by a series of crises of its own, had little will to immerse itself in the affairs of its belligerent neighbor. Left to go their own way, Gaelic and Anglo-Irish elements learned to live together. This would change in the sixteenth century with the ascendancy of Henry VIII.

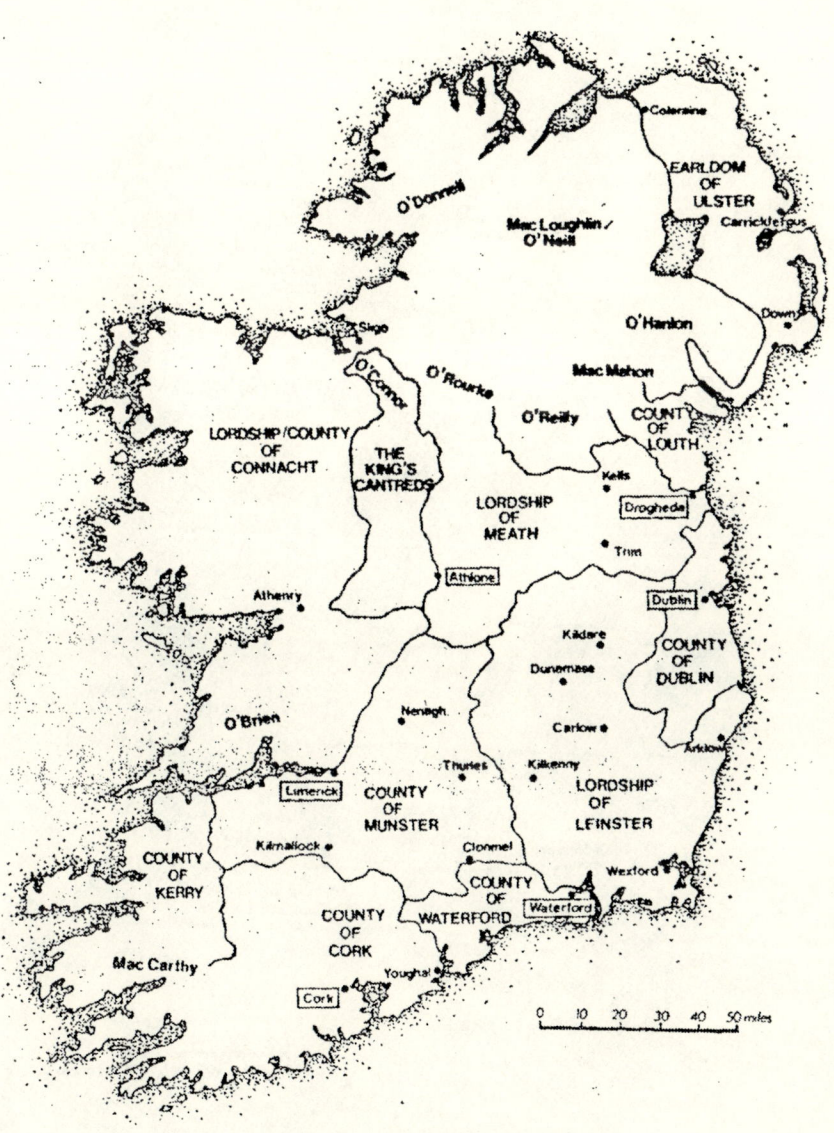

Map of Colonial Ireland c. 1240 A.D.

Celtic Ireland West of the River Shannon

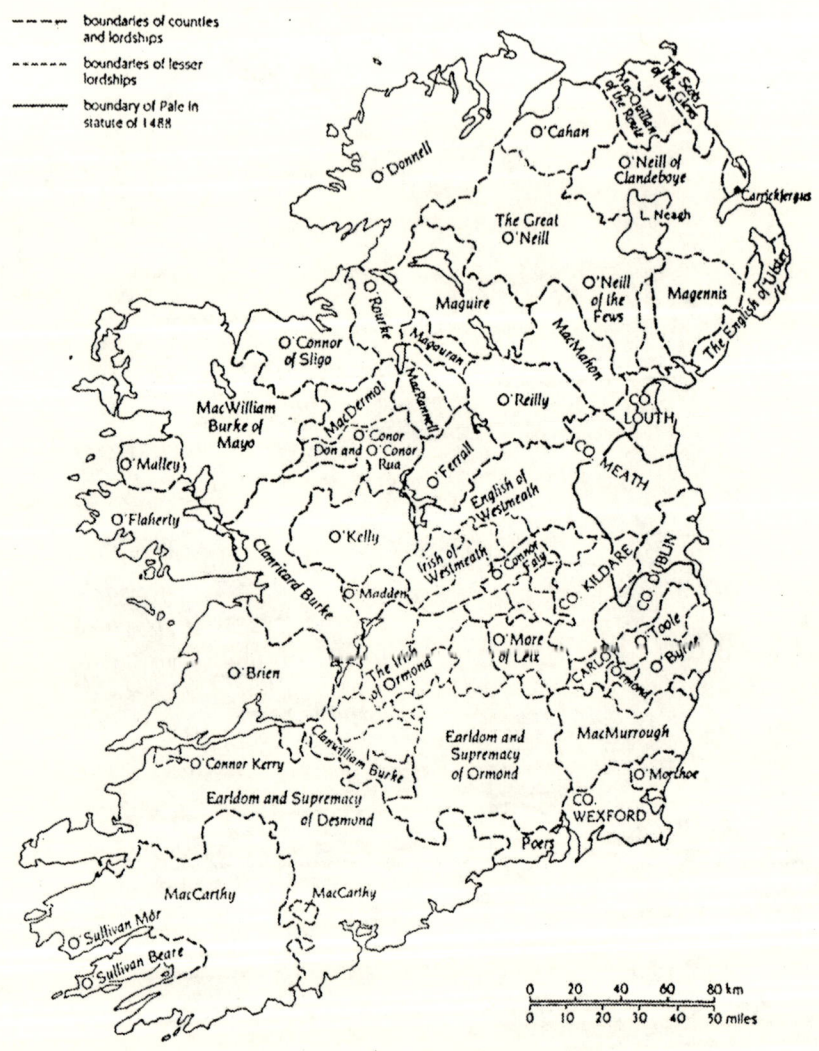

Map of Late Fifteenth Century Ireland
Showing Territorial Boundaries of Major Clans

7

Ancient Ireland West of the River Shannon

The kings of Connacht were already getting their second wind when the ancestors of modern European royalty were still anonymous in the Dark Ages.

—MacDermot of Moylurg

Connacht, Ireland's most western province, remained culturally Celtic longer than any other part of Ireland. It was essentially in Connacht that many features of the Celtic way of life endured well into the seventeenth century, despite heavy incursions by the Anglo-Normans from the late twelfth century onward.

In early times, much of the area, stretching from the River Shannon in the east to the Atlantic seaboard in the west, was known as coiced (meaning fifth) Ol nEcmacht before it was given its present name sometime in the seventh century. It was an area long inhabited by an aboriginal people, generally referred to by ethnologists as Iberian.[53] They held on until the coming of the first Celtic tribes who fought with, but did not enslave, and eventually integrated with them. In turn, the earlier Celtic colonists were overtaken by other Celtic colonizers known as the Gaels, who eventually dominated the aboriginal and earlier Celtic tribes and, in the process, reduced many of them to a subsidiary status. Those powerful enough to maintain a substantial degree of sovereignty within their well-established territories coexisted with the new rulers. As a result of the inescapable assimilation, it became difficult to distinguish with certainty who belonged to which people.

Emerging from this obscure period, historians have been able to identify numerous tribal communities scattered throughout Connacht. Claudius Ptolemy,[54] for example, suggests that a tribe he calls the Auterii populated the coastal regions of present-day counties Galway and Mayo. Other pre-Gael Celts inhabiting the region into historical times were the Gregraige, a Belgae (Firbolg) tribe that occupied much of the western part of present day County Sligo between Loch Gara and the Ox mountains. Others sharing the same area were the Galioin (or Gailenga) and the Luigne tribes of the Laginian tribal family from which the O'Haras, O'Garas and kinfolk are descended. The Ciarrage tribes, sometimes referred to as the "black people," populated much of present-day northwestern County Roscommon and are believed to have been the early lords of Airtech, an area corresponding to the present-day barony of Frenchpark. Their tribal seat was believed to be at Baslic near Castlerea.[55]

The Calraige, another important tribe, had lands in Sligo and Mayo and north Roscommon. They may have been the ancestors of the McGreevy rulers of Moylurg, who were in later times absorbed by the expanding Sil Murray (later the MacDermots) dynasty. It is believed that the territory of the descendants of Oilill Olum, who ruled Connacht in the late fifth century, was to the north of Moylurg in present-day Tirerrill barony in County Sligo. Another powerful federation of tribes was the Ui Maine (O'Kelly), whose extensive territory embraced large areas of what is now south Roscommon, east Galway and north Clare.

According to O'Rahilly, the Ui Maine were either of Firbolg or Laginian origin, who were later given a fictitious Gael pedigree showing them descended from Eochu through his son, Maine Mor. Notwithstanding their notability, O'Rahilly points out that they were vassals who paid tribute to the Gael kings of Connacht. Living among the Ui Maine were the Sogain, a Cruthin (Pict) tribe, and the Dal-na-Druithne.[56]

LEGENDARY RULERS

Among Connacht's legendary rulers of ancient times was the warrior queen, Meave, whose feats are revealed in the *Táin Bó Cualgne*, the central epic of the Ulster Cycle of tales. Meave, upon discovering that her possessions matched those of her husband Ailill, except for a white-horned bull, resolved to make up the deficiency by gaining possession of the most famous bull in the land, the Donn of Cooley, belonging to an Ulster chieftain named Daire. Meave, upon being told that she cannot obtain a loan of the bull, determines to take the animal by force and gathers an army of her Connacht men to invade Ulster.

Due to the temporary impairment which had befallen the Ulster warriors, a youthful warrior named Cu Chulainn undertakes to combat Meave's army single-handedly, fighting one Connacht warrior each day over a period extending from *Samain* (Hallowe'en) until the start of spring. The men of Connacht finally succeeded in invading Ulster and carried off the Bull of Cooley. Overcoming their malaise, the Ulsterman later defeated the men of Connacht. After slaying the White-Horned of Connacht, the Bull of Cooley returns to his native district and "utters mad bellowings of triumph till his heart bursts and he dies."[57]

Another legendary ruler of Connacht was a king by the name of Eochaidh Feidleach who ruled in the pre-Christian era. He built the great palace at Rathcroghan from where one of his descendants, Fearadach, is mentioned in the *Annals* as having ruled in 75 A.D. Fearadach's son, Fiacha, was killed at Magh Cru during the revolt of the Aitheach Tuathar Attacotti. As the story is told, the Attacotti decided it was time to take revenge against their oppressive Gael rulers. They secretly planned a death-feast and invited Fiacha, his chieftains and supporters. During the feast the insurgents attacked the guests and massacred all, including Fiacha. Fiacha was succeeded by his son, Felim, the father of the celebrated Conn of the Hundred Battles, a somewhat legendary ruler, who reigned as high king in the early sagas of the Tara kings.

The Rise of Connacht's Dynastic Tribes

The early genealogists trace the genealogy of Connacht's dynastic tribes to Eochaidh Mugmedon who ruled the province before he became the high king at Tara, where he died in 365 A.D. Mugmedon's grandfather was Cormac Mac Airt, who was a grandson of Conn. His dynastic headquarters is believed to have been at Cruachan in present-day County Roscommon.

Eochaidh Mugmedon had four sons: Brian, Fiachra, Ailill and Niall. The mother of the first three was Mongfionn; Niall's mother was Carthann, the daughter of a British king. According to legend, Carthann gave birth to Niall out on the "plain of Tara" while being pursued by a jealous Mongfionn. It is told that "she did not dare take the child with her; she left it there exposed to the birds. And none of the men of Ireland dared take it for fear of Mongfionn, so great was her magic power and so great the dread she inspired." Then the bard Torna came and rescued the infant revealing to him his destiny: "Seven and twenty years you will rule over Ireland and you will be heir to Ireland for ever."

When Mugmedon became high king in 358 A.D., the Connacht kingship went to Mongfionn's brother Criomhthan. Resentful of this fact, Mongfionn poisoned her brother so that her son Brian could be crowned. Niall, his father's favorite, was made king instead. Only after Niall assumed the high kingship did Brian accede to the kingship of Connacht. Brian was killed (allegedly by his nephew Daithi) in a battle near Tuam. Then, Daithi became king and ruled Connacht until he assumed the high kingship in 405 A.D. Amalgaid succeeded Daithi; in turn, Oilill Molt succeeded Amalgaid. In his attempt to seize the high kingship from the Ui Neills, Oilill was killed at the battle of Ocha, County Meath, in 480 A.D.

In the centuries that followed, the offspring of Brian, Fiachra and Ailill parted into separate dynasties: Ui Briuin, Ui Fiachra and Ui Aillela. Brian's sons or descendents founded three principal dynasties: The Ui Briuin Ali, ancestors of the O'Conors and MacDermots; the Ui Briuin Breifne, precursor of the O'Rourkes of Breifne; and the Ui Briuin Seola, forerunner of the O'Flahertys of West Connacht.

Fiachra, the second brother, founded the Ui Fiachra. Until about the end of the seventh century, the Ui Fiachra appear to have been more powerful than the Ui Briuin Ali. Then they began to break up into geographical septs: in the north of the province in the vicinity of the River Moy (later the barony of Tireragh), their principal residual sept became the O'Dowds; and in the south, what now corresponds to the diocese of Kilmacduagh, were the Ui Fiachrach Aidne (where their best known leader was the renowned Guaire of Kinvara, ruler of Connacht in the middle of the seventh century). Their descendents were the O'Hynes.

The youngest brother Niall moved across the Shannon into Meath where he ruled at Tara. Two of Niall's sons moved north: Conaill into Donegal where he established the Connell clan from whom the O'Donnells are descended; Eoghan to the peninsula now known as Inishowen, from where his descendents moved to what is now Tyrone, where they founded the dynasty of the northern O'Neills.

Over the next few centuries, the Ui Briuin Ali and the Ui Fiachra emerged to dominate the rest of the Connacht tribes so that, by the year 700 A.D., the power structures that would persist in northern Connacht for the next 800 years had begun to form. Throughout the seventh and eighth centuries, Connacht kings were chosen from one or the other branch of these two dynasties. King Aedh of the Ui Briuin ruled until his death in 577 A.D. Thereafter, King Colman of the Ui

Fiachra ruled until Aedh's son Rogallach seized the kingship at the Battle of Canbo in 622 A.D. Later it belonged to Guiare who captured it for the Ui Fiachra. Under Muiredach Mullethan (697–702 A.D.), the leadership reverted to the Ui Briuin Ali. From him the O'Conors and MacDermots and their kinsmen derive the dynastic name of Sil Muiredaigh (Sil Murray), and from then on the descriptions Ui Briuin Ali and Sil Murray became synonymous as the descendents of Muiredach, who consolidated their predominance throughout Connacht.

From the ninth century forward, the Sil Murray were the indisputable rulers. The Ui Fiachra and other earlier ruling tribes lost power, became fragmented, or disappeared as tribal units altogether. Many of the lesser tribes were forced into subsidiary status as the predatory Sil Murray pushed across the province. The homeland of the Ui Briuin Ali was Magh Ai, the great central plain, which is present-day Roscommon. Cruachan was the royal residence until somewhere about the seventh century when it seems to have been abandoned as such. Duma Shelca, near Carn Froach (Carnfree) in Roscommon, became the site of the royal dwelling and inauguration site of the Connacht kings.

THE RISE OF THE O'CONOR DYNASTY

The most significant of the Sil Murray clan were the O'Conors, who took their name from Conor, who ruled as King of Connacht from 966–971 A.D. Conor's brother Mulrooney was given Moylurg, a territory matching present-day Boyle barony in North Roscommon. There, he founded an independent sept or tuath, which became known after him as O Mulrooney. Later, the sept adopted the surname MacDermot, after Dermot who held the kingship of Moylurg from 1124–1159.

In 1106, Turlough Mor O'Conor deposed his brother Donal as Sil Murray King of Connacht and went on to become high king in 1119. He died in 1156, leaving behind a large family of twenty-three sons. After endless squabbles among his heirs, the eldest son Rory emerged as his successor. Rory was high king of Ireland when the Anglo-Normans invaded the country in 1169. It was Rory with whom King Henry II negotiated the Treaty of Windsor in 1175. The Treaty granted Rory the kingship of Connacht and the high-kingship of the non-Norman areas of Ireland and, in return, he agreed to pay Henry an annual tribute. Eleven years later in 1186, Rory was ousted from the kingship by his son Conor. Rory then retired to the monastery of Cong where he died in 1198. Cathal Crobhderg, son of Turlough Mor, became king of Connacht in 1201. He was inaugurated at Carnfree near Tulsk in an imposing ceremony recorded by Donough O'Mulconroy, an eyewitness at the ceremony. What O'Mulconroy recorded (reproduced below) tells us much about the more important families in thirteenth century Connacht, and the role each was assigned in discharging the king's duties:

> "This is the lawful form of inauguration of the king of Connaught, as it was established in the olden time, and ordained by Saint Patrick on the day that he inaugurated Duach Galach, and on which occasion he was assisted by twelve bishops. And it is necessary that the successors of these bishops should be present at his inauguration, namely the successor of Saint Patrick at Elphin, the successor of Saint Bridget at Ballintuber, the successor of Dachonna of Asmacnerk (now Assylinn), the successor of Saint Beo-Aedh of Ardcarn, the successor of Barry at Clooncorby (now Kilbarry), the successor of Saint Colman of Mayom, the successor of Saint Giallan of Moygillen, the successor of Bishop Sechell of Lough Salchern, the successor of Saint Grellan of Creeve, the successor of Saint Callin of Fenagh, the successor of Saint Finian of Cloncraff.
>
> "It was also ordained that the twelve dynasts or sub-chiefs of Connaught should be present at this inauguration, namely, O'Flannagan, O'Mulrenin, O'Finaghty and Mageraghty (who were called the four royal chieftains of the King of Connaught); O'Flynn, O'Hanley, O'Fallon, O'Beirne, O'Concannon, O'Heyne, O'Shaughnessy and O'Teighe, who was chief of the household of the King of Connaught.

"It was also required that the following chiefs should be present at his installation, namely, O'Rourke, O'Reilly, O'Hara and O'Gara, with their followers and McDermot, chief of Moylurg.

"It is the privilege of O'Mulconroy to place the rod in the hands of O'Conor, the day on which he assumes the sovereignty of Connaught, and it is considered unlawful that any man should be along with the King on the carn except O'Mulconroy and O'Connaghten fronting O'Mulconroy, or more truly fronting O'Mulrenin, who kept the entrance of the carn.

"The King's clothing and arms were given to O'Mulconroy and his steed to O'Flynn the coarb of Saint Dachonna, who was privileged to mount that steed from O'Conor's back. An ounce of gold was decreed to O'Connaghten as a perennial tribute, on condition of his repairing the carn when it required repairs. The following are the subsidies paid to the different chieftains of Sil Murray by O'Conor, King of Connaught. Twelve score milch cows, twelve score sheep, and twelve score cows to O'Flannagan, and the same number to Mageraghty and O'Mulrenin. The office of the High Steward to O'Conor was ceded to O'Flannagan, O'Hanley is the keeper of his hostages and he had the command of his fleet from Slieve-in-Iarain to Luinnech (Limerick) with all the perquisites thereupon belonging. MacBranan is henchman, and chief of his kerne, and the caretaker of his hounds. MacDockwra is his procurator-general who is bound to furnish light and bedding. It is the duty of O'Flannagan, O'Beirne and MacDockwra to guard the spoils of O'Conor, whenever he encamps to rest. MacBranan has the perquisites arising from O'Conor's marchership, from Curragh-Kinnetty (near Roscommon) to Kells in Meath; O'Flynn the marchership in the tract extending from Curragh-Kinnetty to Croagh Patrick, together with its stewardship.

"The chief command of O'Conor's fleet belongs to O'Flaherty and O'Malley. O'Kelly is the chief treasure of his precious stones, and all other species of treasure. MacDermot of Moylurg is his marshal; O'Teige the chief of his household; O'Beirne his chief butler; O'Finaghty his chief doorkeeper; O'Mulconry the recorder of all his tributes; MacTully his physician, and MacEgan his brehon (judge).

"Twenty-four townlands constitute the lawful patrimony of each of these eight chiefs, in payment of the offices they discharge for O'Conor. Forty-eight townlands, constituted the patrimony of each of his four royal chiefs, O'Flannagan, O'Mulrenin, Mageraghty and O'Finaghty, together with all dead Church lands.

"The chiefs tributary to O'Conor were those of Galenga Costello, Clann Cuan, Conmairne, Carra, and the two Leynies. In short, there was not a king, or royal heir, or chieftain of a cantred, or a district, or a hundred-cattled farmer of a townland from Assaroe to Luinne (Limerick) and from Uisnech in Meath to Inish-Boffenne, and from Lough Eren to Lough Deirgherc, who was not specially bound to attend with his forces at the hostings of O'Conor.

"The free states of Connaught are the following, namely, Ui-Bruin of Brefney, the Ui-Fiachrach of the Moy, and the race of Muiredhach, son of Fergus, and even of these, notwithstanding their freedom, two are bound to attend with their forces at the hostings of O'Conor, and to assist him in all his troubles and difficulties."[58]

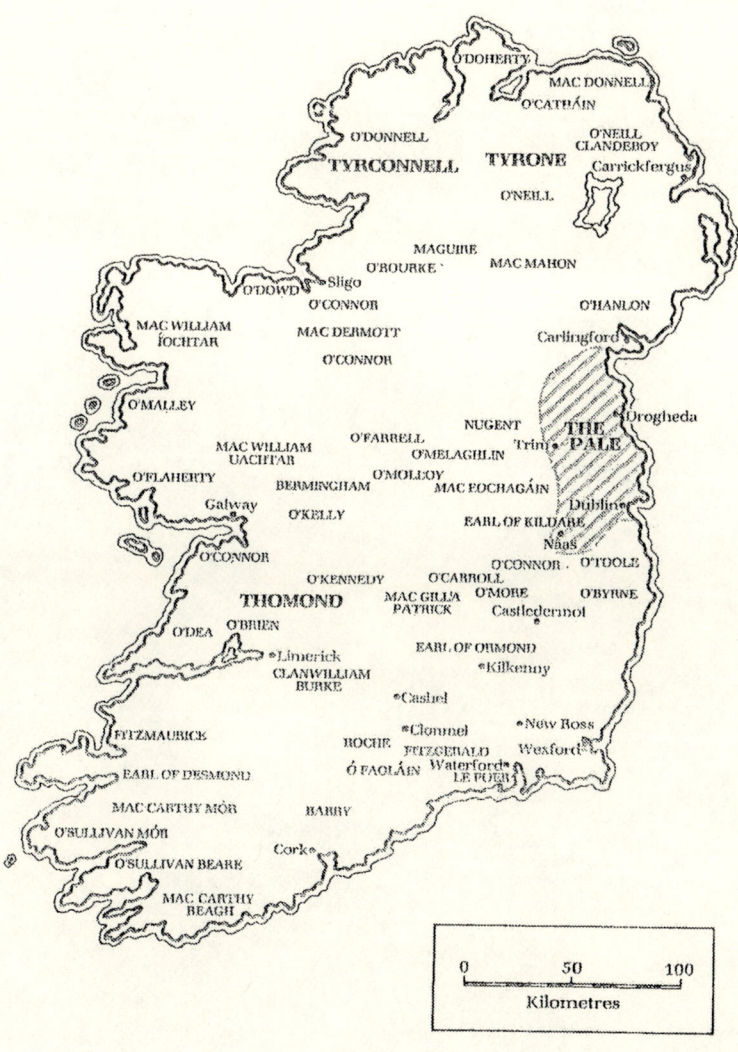

Map of Ireland Showing
Lordships of the Later Middle Ages

8

Anglo-Norman Colonization of Connacht

> Connacht, already too familiar with the evils of domestic strife, was plunged into ceaseless warfare on a vaster scale than it had hitherto known, a condition of things which was to last for hundreds of years to come.
>
> —G. Moran and R. Gillespie, eds.,
> *Galway: History and Society* (1996)

A new chapter was unveiled in the history of Connacht in the late twelfth century when the O'Conors, weakened in their warring ability from endless conflict with their kinsmen and neighbors, fell prey to invading Anglo-Norman barons. The first of the Normans to arrive in Connacht was Milo de Cogan, invited there in 1177 by Conor Maenmoy, who did it to upset his father Rory. Upon hearing of his son's betrayal, Rory took after him and poked out his eyes. But what was done could not be undone, and Conor Maenmoy's invitation threw open the door for the adventurous Normans who at the time were in search of new lands for themselves in Connacht.

Not too many years later, in 1193, the first Norman colony was established in Connacht when Gilbert de Nangle entered the service of Cathal O'Conor. De Nangle was rewarded with lands in the area of Loughrea. After that, Cathal used the Norman barons repeatedly in his encounters with rival kinsmen. In 1201, he was instrumental in bringing in the first of the de Burghs and, thereafter, the history of the western province and the fortunes of the O'Conors and the de Burghs became inextricably linked.

King Rory O'Conor died in 1198 and a bitter family dispute for his successor followed. His brother, Cathal Crobhderg, emerged as king in 1215. Cathal died in 1224 and succession was again bitterly contested by Rory's heirs who ravaged the countryside in the process.

With some support from the Normans (who encouraged conflict among the Gaelic chieftains), Cathal's eldest son Aedh succeeded in assuming the kingship. Cathal's challengers were Turlough and another Aedh (sons of the former King Rory), and together they declared all-out warfare against him. However, Aedh managed to hold onto the kingship until he got himself killed, not on the battlefield, but at home in a bathtub. As the story goes, he was having a bath with a carpenter's wife when her husband came upon them and, in a fit of anger, grabbed an ax and hacked the misfortunate Aedh to death.[59]

The other Aedh then seized the kingship, but in 1232 Felim (another son of Cathal Crobhderg) was made king. Felim O'Conor died in 1265 and his son, yet another Aedh, succeeded him as king of Connacht. According to the annalists, this Aedh fought both Normans and Gaels indiscriminately at every opportunity he could get. He married Ailin, a daughter of Dugald MacSorley of a great Scottish galloglass family, and came back in 1259 with her dowry of eight score professional well-armed and well-trained mercenary warriors (known as galloglasses) from the Western Isles of Scotland. This was the first band of galloglasses to appear in Connacht, and many more would follow to help the Gaelic chieftains in their struggles against the Anglo-Normans and with each other.

Aedh died in 1274 and in the fifty years following his death there were no fewer than fourteen successive O'Conor kings of Connacht, of whom only one died a natural death. The Normans killed one O'Conor king at the battle of Athenry, and the others were all either killed or disposed of by their own kinsmen.[60]

The Founding of a Norman Colony

William de Burgh, the founder of the de Burgh dynasty in Connacht, is believed to have arrived in Ireland with Prince John in 1185, at which time he was given a grant of land in Munster. At a later date, Prince John, in what appeared to be a violation of the Treaty of Windsor (1175),[61] made a tentative grant of much of Connacht to this same William de Burgh who, in turn, regranted ten cantreds in the north of Connacht to his compatriot Hugh de Lacy. This course of action plunged a Connacht already torn apart with domestic strife into a situation of relentless warfare on a more extensive scale than it had hitherto experienced, a situation which was to last for some generations to come.[62]

Richard de Burgh succeeded his father William and in 1215 he received from King John a new grant of Connacht similar to that made to his father. Henry III made this grant official in 1224 when he gave Richard title to most of the province (twenty-five cantreds in all). However, Henry reserved for himself a large part of what is now County Roscommon and small portions of Galway and Sligo. The area, described as the heartland of O'Conor country, consisted of five cantreds: the Three Tuaths, Moylurg, Omany, Tirmany, and Magh-Ai.

Richard moved with haste to establish a firm Norman foothold, parceling out large tracts of land to fellow-Norman barons and establishing rule over the existing society and economy. He seized for himself the rich land of Galway between Loch Corrib and the Shannon, while a fellow-Norman, Maurice Fitzgerald, took most of Sligo and the lands of O hEidhin in South Galway. Many others, such as the Berminghams, Prendergasts, Stauntons, de Exeters and de Angulos (later Costellos), were also the recipients of large tracts of land.

Richard de Burgh left no stone unturned to secure control of his region. He kept up the pressure everywhere, overrunning a great part of the province and seizing large territories, including those of the

O'Flaherties and the O'Hallorans who were driven across the Corrib River into the wild mountainous region of Connemara. His dream of making himself virtual master of Connacht was realized in 1228 when he was made justiciar. The annalists point out that his task was made easier by the continued domestic conflicts of the O'Conors, the only people who might have effectively resisted him.[63]

Richard de Burgh, to whom (rather than his father) the title of "Conqueror of Connacht" should belong, did more than conquer the land of the O'Conors; he planted it extensively. From 1237 onwards, he brought in a new class of proprietors or local rulers who, in the course of a century, turned the province into what was virtually an Anglo-Norman and Welsh colony[64] in which the de Burghs were to all intents and purposes its King.

DECLINE OF THE O'CONOR DYNASTY

Later in the century, Henry IV (successor to Henry III), having come to terms with Felim O'Conor, leased the royal territory (five cantreds) to him in exchange for a rental fee to the English crown. Felim recognized that this arrangement, in effect, partitioned Connacht between himself and de Burgh (the latter of course getting the lion's share), but each as a tenant of the Crown at a determined rent.

Felim and his successors continued to claim the whole of their original inheritance and use of the title of King of Connacht, but it was now an empty phrase since their jurisdiction from this time on was confined to the five cantreds, a district which, as time went by, was still further reduced in size by the loss of Omany and Timany.

Felim reigned from 1233–1265. After his death, his son Aedh assumed the kingship. The annalists characterize him as a brutal leader even by the barbarous mores of the times. He was consistently hostile to the Normans and waged many battles against them, the most successful in 1270 when he routed a large de Burgh armed force at Ath-an-Chip (near present-day Carrick-on-Shannon). It is said that he was a compulsive killer, and among his favorite targets were the O'Rourkes of Breifne. When he died in 1274, his obituary in the *Annals of Connacht* described him as follows:

"Aedh son of Felim son of Cathal Crobhderg, King of Connacht for nine years, died on the third day of May this year, a Thursday and the feast of the Invention of the Holy Cross; a king who wasted and desolated Connacht in fighting the Galls and Gaels who opposed him; a king who inflicted great defeats on the Galls and pulled down their palaces and castles; a king who took the hostages of the Ui Briuin and the Cenel Conaill; the destroyer and healer of Ireland was he; the king most dreaded and triumphant of all the kings of Ireland in his day."[65]

In the fifty years following Aedh's death, there were no fewer than fourteen successive O'Conor kings of Connacht, and throughout all this time the unrestrained Gaelic chieftains engaged in endless warring among themselves and with the Normans. By the end of the thirteenth century, war had reached the pandemic stage, contributing in part to an exodus from the land that was causing a significant shortfall in income to the Crown. Official documents of the period show that the O'Conors, de Burghs and others had fallen greatly behind in their remuneration to the Crown, which could not be collected because the country was completely drained from the endless hostilities everywhere.

"More Irish Than the Irish Themselves"

By the fourteenth century, the de Burghs had become "more Irish than the Irish themselves." Richard de Burgh died in 1326 and was succeeded by his grandson William, only a boy of fourteen at the time. Seven years later, his assassination by a kinsman was regarded as a turning point in the history of Anglo-Norman power in Ireland, resulting in a sweeping overthrow of the established system of administration throughout Connacht. Within fifty years, the province was once again in the hands of the Gaelic princes and was not re-conquered until the close of the Tudor period.

In the meantime, William's infant daughter and heiress Elizabeth was taken to England where she later married Lionel, son of Edward III, thus conveying the de Burgh Lordship of Connacht (and Ulster) to the Royal House of England. This conveyance was little more than technical and, in actual practice, the estate of Elizabeth passed to her cousins, William and Edmund, to whom it seemed unacceptable that an absentee should rule in the Irish lands of de Burgh. So they agreed to divide Elizabeth's inheritance between them with William taking the upper portion that included the town and county of Galway and Edmond taking the lower comprised mainly of County Mayo.

They withdrew their allegiance to the English Crown and assumed Irish names: William calling himself MacWilliam Upper and Edmond MacWilliam Lower. Other Normans followed suit, embracing the Irish language and dress and becoming in all walks of life independent Gaelic chieftains. Hence, the Norman-Irish succeeded the Anglo-Norman colony, and all efforts of the Crown to win back its loyalty were in vain. At this point, it is worth mentioning that the Norman ascendancy in Connacht (in its later phase rightly called Anglo-Norman) was relatively short-lived, but it left an enduring legacy on the region's culture and institutions.

GALWAY: THE MAKING OF A MEDIEVAL TRADING CENTER

The de Burghs selected the site of Galway on the Atlantic coast as their chief seat, building a castle on the site of an earlier O'Flaherty fortification. Before the arrival of the Anglo-Normans, this area belonged to the O'Hallorans and was protected by their overlords, the O'Flaherties, for the O'Conor kings. For a time, the O'Flaherties successfully resisted de Burghs' efforts to build on the site until 1232 when Richard de Burgh routed the O'Flaherties, forcing their leader Hugh O'Flaherty out of Galway. A year later, Felim O'Conor lay siege to the site, captured the "castle" and demolished de Burgh's annexation.

Richard de Burgh regained the site and shortly thereafter built a new castle around which a fortified community evolved. In 1270, the de Burghs began enclosing the site with walls and by the early fourteenth century, a traditional Norman model town (described by some as "the remotest town in European civilization") had emerged. In 1312, the town walls were strengthened by the erection of the "great gate" and other substantial fortifications.

However, the early years in the new colony were anything but calm as the de Burghs struggled continuously to keep the beleaguered post from being recaptured by the natives. Again and again, the Gaelic chieftains pushed hard to recapture this vital spot and though they did not succeed, they at least made the tenure of the Norman inhabitants a costly one.

Many historians are convinced that Galway owes its impetus more to the achievements of a number of families that settled there during the thirteenth and fourteenth centuries than to the de Burghs. In all, there were fourteen families: Athy, Blake, Bodkin, Brown, Deane, Darcy, Font, French, Joyce, Kirwin, Lynch, Martin, Morris and Skerrett. These became known as the "Tribes of Galway." There were other families of course, but the "Tribe" families came to be easily the most important of the newcomers and of them the Lynches were the most important, contributing much to the culture and political economy of the city.

In 1484, it was Domnick Lynch who received the city's charter under Richard III. His son Stephan received the "Wardenship" of Galway from Pope Innocent VIII. James Lynch became notorious when, as mayor in 1493, he presided at the hanging of his own son. One or two of the "Tribes" were of Gaelic extraction, but most belonged to those Norman and Welsh families who were introduced into the western province mainly by Richard de Burgh. The "Tribes" were in fact aristocratic conquistadors and landed gentry who exchanged their swords for ledgers and turned to commerce as a career. In a relatively short period, they had evolved into a powerful oligarchy of merchant princes, turning the town of Galway into virtually a city-state.

TRADE AND COMMERCE

Within two centuries of the arrival of the Anglo-Normans, Galway had evolved from an obscure village to an important seaport with trade contacts throughout western Europe. Many attribute this shift almost entirely to the merchant community that had advanced themselves into an oligarchy that directed the town's commerce and ran its government.

Galway had become an important export and import center by the fifteenth century, importing wine and other commodities and exporting wool, sheepskins, hides, cattle, linen and a host of other materials.[66] The rapidly expanding wool trade with merchants from Italy and Flanders made the raising of sheep and the export of wool a lucrative business and, according to some sources, wool (more than any other export) contributed to the prosperity of the community. While the Italian merchants were foremost in the wool trade with Ireland, they were paramount in the field of banking and money lending. Church dignitaries, nobles and merchants were accustomed to looking to Italian banks and lending institutions to borrow money, and Connacht was no exception. Even among the landed classes, money was regularly raised on the security of property to facilitate domestic projects.[67]

Wine, a beverage long favored by the Irish, was imported from France as far back as the pre-Christian era. After the country embraced Christianity, its need for wine for religious services made its use more common. When the Normans arrived in the twelfth century, their preference for the beverage further enhanced its demand. As the commercial policy of Ireland at this period depended to a great extent on the dictates of the Crown, it was therefore normal that most of the wine imported into the country should come from the King's dominions in France.

However, this monopoly by the French wine merchants began to crack in the latter part of the fourteenth century when a new commercial policy enacted in England undermined the French wine merchant's exclusive shipping privileges. About the same time the Anglo-Normans of Connacht, having abandoned their allegiance and switched over completely to the Gaelic order, petitioned Richard II to allow merchants from the Spanish peninsula to traffic freely with Ireland. With the King's consent, a new and lucrative trade opened for Connacht, as merchants from Lisbon and Portugal began trading freely with Galway.[68]

In the course of the next hundred years, Galway built up a considerable traffic in Spanish wine and merchandise upon which the wealth of the town and its importance as a commercial center grew. In its commercial gravitation towards Spain, Galway is said to have set in motion the first step towards cutting the umbilical cord between the Anglo-Norman colonists in Connacht and the mother country.

END OF GAELIC RULE

Towards the end of the sixteenth century, the Crown made several attempts to restore law and order throughout the province. Connacht was divided into shires, sheriffs were appointed, and provision was made for judicial review. Change, however, did not come about easily. Another attempt was made at stopping the endless tribal feuding in 1585 when the Compossicion of Connacht was introduced, albeit unsuccessfully, to supplant the Gaelic Brehon Code with the English legal and administrative system.

Further attempts by the Crown to extend control over non-compliance areas thrust Connacht into another cycle of warfare. Incessant warfare and hostility between the great families of Connacht took its toll and hastened the break-up of the Gaelic aristocracy. The defeat of Irish and Spanish forces at the Battle of Kinsale in 1602, followed thereafter by the plantation of parts of Ulster with Scots and English settlers, led to great political and social upheaval. Following England's Civil War in 1653, a series of Acts passed by the Cromwellian parliament decreed that Irish landowners were to be transplanted into Connacht. This led to massive confiscation throughout the province to accommodate the transplantees.

For his part in siding with the royalists in the Civil War, the O'Conor Don lost his castle at Ballintubber and much of his lands east of the River Suck, including the town of Castlerea which went to Captain Theophilus Sandford for his services in the War. For the O'Conors, it was the final chapter of one of Connacht's great Gaelic families, whose power and prestige had dominated the western province for more than seven centuries.

Map of Thirteenth Century Connacht Showing
De Burgh Lordship and the Five Cantreds of the King

9

Historical Tuaths of Eastern Connacht

ooooooooooooooooooooooooo

Let us commemorate the Three Tuaths,
the steady forces of fair Cruachan;
Let us not spoil their untarnished splendour,
let us name their three lords.
Brave are the defending tribe of Muintir Beirne
in the fortress of O Monaghan.
Through conflict, vigor and threatening,
theirs is the country into which they came.
Powerful is the vigor of Clann Brennan,
and also of the majestic O Mulmihil
They command the strong forces of Corca Achlann of the herds
Hereditary to the keen-armed O hAinlighe,[69]
in Cenel Dobtha, the fast rugged
I have affection for them in my heart.
They are the clan of O hAinlighe.[70]

—Topographical Poems of John O'Dubhagain, c. 1320

Long before Ireland was organized into parishes and counties, there were territorial sub-divisions of which the smallest having its own political and legal administration was the tuath. Originally, the term meant a "tribe of people" before it eventually came to be known as the territory occupied by the tribe. Each tuath was considered akin to an area having thirty *ballys* (townlands) each of which, according to Brehon law, was of sufficient acreage to sustain three hundred cows "without one cow touching the other."

There were scores of tuaths, or petty kingdoms, in early Ireland. They were loosely joined together in clusters of three or four into local kingdoms that, in turn, were grouped with several other kingdoms to form an over- or provincial-kingdom under the predominance of a royal over-king. These over-kings had no direct sway over the internal affairs of the petty kingdoms under their over-lordship, but they could summon contingents from their sub-kingdoms to support their causes and partake in their battles. For instance, the scribes tell us that in 1172 Roderick O'Connor, King of Connacht, finding that King Henry II had given his Norman lord, Hugh de Lacy, possession of the Kingdom of Meath, assembled a large army from the sub-kingdoms of Connacht with which he advanced on Trim Castle in Leinster and burned it to the ground.

In this entirely decentralized society where no one central leader commanded final authority for exacting compliance of the law, but where disputes were common, there was an influential class of legal scholars called brehons in whose hands rested the interpretation of the complicated legal rules set forth in the *Brehon Law Books*.

THE THREE TUATHS

In the province of Connacht, there were some thirty tuaths. Among them were three known collectively as the Tri Tuaths and separately as Tir-Briuin-na-Sionna, Kinel Dofa and Corca Eachlinn. They were located on the west side of the River Shannon in present-day County Roscommon and their overall boundary stretched from Lanesboro in the south, past Elphin to the west, to Jamestown in the north, and back again along the west bank of the River Shannon.[71] The earliest inhabitants of the area are believed to have been the Gowanree, a fierce Firbolg tribe, who ruled the area until well into the early historical period. Subsequently, the Gowanree withdrew into virtual obscurity before emerging again several centuries later as the territorial chieftains of Mura na Manachain, an area compared to the present-day parishes of Aughrim, Kilmore and Cloncraft. Sharkey, in *Heart of Ireland* (1927), describes these people as small in stature, with dark hair and complexion, and having bowed legs from riding horses. (Interestingly, Sharkey's description fits that of the Celts of the Iberian peninsula where they intermarried with the indigenous population.) One of their strongholds, he writes, was atop Sliabh Baghna[72] (more commonly called Slieve Bawn), a ridge dividing Kinel Dofa from Corca Eachlinn.

Among the most important families linked to the Three Tuaths throughout much of the Gaelic period were O'Monaghan and O'Beirne in Tir-Briuin-na-Sionna, O'Hanley in Kinel Dofa, and Mulvihills and MacBrennans in Corca Eachlinn. Their respective ancestral roots stretch back to very early times. The question arises, however, as to which branch of the Celtic family these families belonged. Some genealogists suggest that the MacBrennans, O'Hanlys, O'Monaghans, O'Beirnes and some of their immediate neighbors were remnants of Fir Bolg tribes that had ruled the region at an earlier date, suggesting that throughout Connacht, as elsewhere in Ireland, the interstices between the major dynasties were filled with minor kingdoms and vassal peoples who previously had ruled large portions of the province before the rise of the Gael colonists.

Other genealogists, however, disagree and link these families to the Ui Briuin dynastic family, believing them to be descendants of Cenel MacErca,[73] a tribe named after its progenitor, Erca, one of King Brian's lesser known sons who settled the territory and called it Tir-Briuin-na-Sinna after his father. According to tradition, the territory was later divided among three of Erca's grandsons, Ona, Ida and Dofa. Ona, from whom it is said the MacBrennans descend, received Corca Eachlinn. Dofa, believed to have been the progenitor of the O'Hanleys, received Kinel Dofa. And Ida presumably received Tir-Briuin-na-Sinna, although there is no obvious confirmation of it. If, as believed by some, O'Hanley and MacBrennan descended from Erca, it would confirm that both septs were related to, but not part of, the Sil Murray dynasty from which the O'Conors, MacDermots and their kinfolk descended. They were descendent from King Brian, but not through the Sil Murray clan.

O'Monaghan, however, does not appear to fit into the mold described for O'Hanley and MacBrennan. Norman Mongan (*The Menapia Quest*, 1975) traces the O'Monaghan pedigree through Mannachan all the way back to Monaig Mor, the eponymous ancestor of the Firbolgs. He believes the sept was given a spurious pedigree linking it with Ui Briuin-na-Sionna. Some genealogists suggest that O'Beirne may have descended from Bjorn, a Norseman chieftain who established a colony on the River Shannon during the Viking era. But it is quite possible that a mixture of Gael and Firbolg blood flowed through all their veins. Verse passed down from the ancient poets proclaims how tribes from the various invaders coexisted and intermarried. Few pre-Gael genealogies have been preserved. In any case, genealogists were constantly inclined to disagree when compiling family pedigrees.

Kingdom of Moylurg

Adjoining the northern boundary of the Three Tuaths was another historic tuath, the Kingdom of Moylurg. The territory of Moylurg, more correctly defined as the two tuaths of Moylurg and Tir-Tuathail (Keadue, Ballyfarnon and Arigna), corresponds roughly to the present barony of Boyle: bounded on the east by the River Shannon; on the north by the Arigna Mountains, Loch Arrow and the Curlews; and on the west by Loch Gara and the Breedogue River. No physical boundary separated it from the Magh Ai of the O'Conors to the south. The tuath of Airtech (roughly Frenchpark, Tibohine and Loughlynn areas) was added later and until the expansion of the Costellos in the thirteenth century, it included Kilcolman and Castlemore in eastern Mayo.

In early times, Clan McGreevy ruled the kingdom of Moylurg. They were overlords of thirty-two tribes known collectively as the Feara Scene or Feara Scedne. Little is known about the Feara Scene except for a reference in the *Annals of Lough Cé* for the year 1238 which records: "Cathal MagRiabhaigh [McGreevy], chieftain of Feara-Scene, mortuus est." Moylurg was the country of an ancient tribe called Calraige that, over the centuries, had been absorbed by the expanding Sil Murray (later MacDermot) clan. MacNiocaill, in *Ireland Before the Vikings*, described the Calraighe of Moylurg as having been "crushed" by the Ui Briuin in 752 A.D. and "slaughtered" by the Ui Fiachrach in 777 A.D. Moylurg's ancient name was Magh Luirg an Dagda, meaning the plain of the tracks of the Dagda, a king of the legendary Tuatha de Danann.[74] O'Dugan's fourteenth century topographical poem, lists MacEoach and MacMaon as well as McGreevy as ancient chiefs of Moylurg.

A shift in tribal power sometime in the twelfth century resulted in Moylurg falling into the hands of the more powerful emerging Sil Murray (MacDermot) clan. How this came about is not altogether clear. The *Annals of Lough Cé* has only a handful of entries referring to the McGreevy clan, and none mention any conflict between them and the McDermots. Neither is there mention of a territorial transition to MacDermot control. An entry for 1105 reads: "MagRiabhaigh (McGreevy), Nial, son of, lord of Callraighe, died," which seems to indicate that the McGreevys were still the chiefs. MacLysaght, in his *More Irish Families,* says that the chiefs of the name of McGreevy were lords of Moylurg until the thirteenth century when they were subdued by, and made tributaries to, the MacDermots. Other references suggest that the MacDermots had acquired Moylurg at an earlier date.

A poem to Tomaltach-an-Einigh MacDermot, King of Moylurg, written by Tuathal O Higgin in c. 1421, recounts the story that following the death of Tadhg of the Towers (Sil Murray King of Connacht from 924–956 A.D.), his sons Conor and Mulrooney made some kind of deal whereby, in return for the territory of Moylurg and other specified tributes, Mulrooney surrendered any claim to the kingship of Connacht in favor of Conor.[75] One can suppose that when the Sil Murray established themselves in Moylurg, the fortunes and misfortunes of the smaller clans throughout the area, McGreevy included, were affected by this powerful clan's expansion and mastery.

THE KING'S CANTREDS

The Three Tuaths and Moylurg, together with the tuaths of Omany, Tirmany and Magh-Ai, were also referred to as the King's (English) Cantreds from 1224. This territory, a narrow strip of land in eastern Connacht stretching from Athlone in the south to Sligo in the north, and corresponding in area to present-day County Roscommon and small portions of Galway and Sligo, was retained by King Henry III for himself in the thirteenth century. He gave title to the remainder of Connacht (twenty-five cantreds in all) to Richard de Burgh who had subjugated the province. This, the heartland of O'Conor country, was a great loss to the powerful Gaelic kings and chieftains of Connacht who had nobody to thank but themselves. They had battled one another barbarously in internecine warfare that wrought havoc everywhere, weakened their fighting ability and in the end caused their own destruction. Later in the century, Henry IV (successor to Henry III), having come to terms with Felim O'Conor, leased the royal territory (five cantreds) to him in exchange for a rental fee to the English crown.

Thus, by a strange paradox, this ruling resulted in the preservation of the Three Tuaths as a Gaelic enclave up to the seventeenth century. It remained an area governed in the broad tradition of the Brehon Code: largely ignored while much of the rest of Ireland was being subdued and colonized; where the lines of ruling families stayed in place on the same lands over countless generations; where the lifestyles, habits, customs and beliefs of the inhabitants remained unchanged for centuries; and much given to tribal feuding and succession disputes.

The Three Tuaths are separately presented in the following chapters for a closer look at the basic territorial units in the Gaelic social structure.

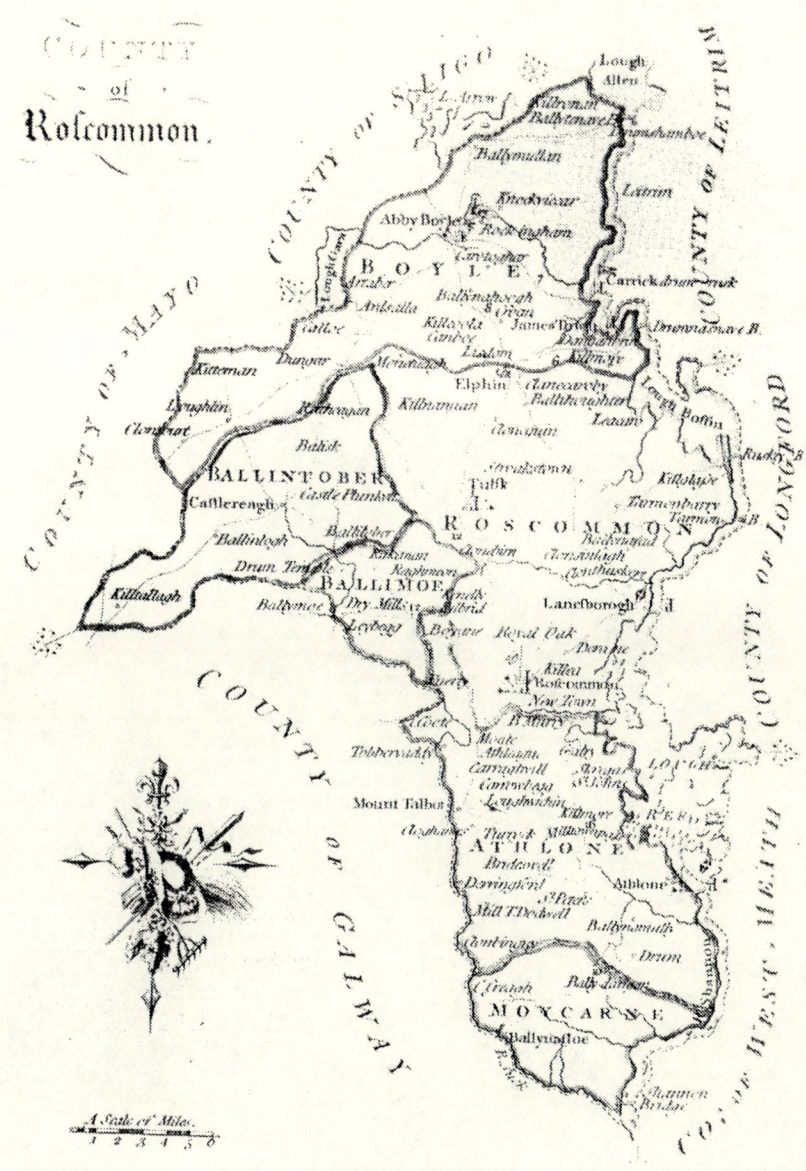

Map of the County of Roscommon
From Scalé's *Hibernian Atlas* (1776)

10

The Three Tuaths—Kinel Dofa

Kinel Dofa was a petty kingdom, part of a Gaelic enclave in eastern Connacht that was remote, lawless and much given to tribal feuding and plundering during much of the Middle Ages. Its area was approximate to the parishes of Kilglass, Termonbarry, Cloontoosket, Kilgefin, the eastern half of Lissonuffy and the townland of North Yard in Bumlin. Located to the south of its sister tuath, Tir-Briuin-na-Sionna, its northern and eastern boundary line extended along the River Shannon from Carranadoe Bridge to Drumdaff at the southern end of Kilgefin parish. Separating it from its other sister tuath, Corca Eachlinn, was the ridge of Slievebawn at its southern line and the Kilglass Lakes to the west. Within its boundaries was the east slope of Slievebawn where, according to tradition, a tribe of Firbolgs eked out a modest living on the hillside adjacent to their Gael neighbors early into the Christian period.

The O'Hanley clan ruled Kinel Dofa. Their chieftain was one of twelve principal officials in charge of the King of Connacht's (O'Conor) Shannon fleet. O'Hanley is said to have descended from King Brian (who ruled Connacht 366–388 A.D.) through Dofa whose grandfather was Eric, the progenitor of Kinel Mac Erca.[76] Throughout the Gaelic era, the Hanleys were important players in the alliance that ruled the three tuaths. They are mentioned many times in the *Annals of the Four Masters* and in other writings. Raghnall, chief of the sept, was killed leading his forces in support of King Brian Boru against the Vikings at the Battle of Clontarf in 1014. His descendent, Donal O'Hanley, was the first of that surname which he adopted from his ancestor, Ainle. He served as Bishop of Dublin from 1085–1095. His nephew, Samuel Hanley, succeeded him and served until 1121.

The O'Hanleys built a great church in the twelfth century at Cluain-Cairpthe (present-day Kilbarry) on the site where their patron Saint Berach (Saint Barry) founded a monastery in the sixth century.[77] John Donovan, visiting the area in 1837, wrote that Cluain Coirpthe would have been an ecclesiastical establishment of great importance in its day. He could identify many of the former buildings from the ruins: Teampull Mor was a very ancient church; Teach Dorch (dark house) was identified as a penitentiary of very ancient architecture without a single window; and Teach Gael (white house) was also identified as a penitentiary, a place where the penitent was allowed to see daylight through a window after he had been through the dark house, "as the holy fathers had done in Limbo before Christ released them from there." He also identified the ruins of Saint Barry's Chapel, the remains of a round tower and a causeway, which extended across the bog from Kilbarry to Newtown.[78]

The monastery graveyard was the burial place of many celebrities down the centuries. Among those listed in the *Annals* as buried there were: Tanaide O' Maelchonaire, *ollav* (man of learning) of the Sil Murray and described as the most skilled man of his profession in his time (1385), Aedh O hAinlidhe, chieftain of Kinel Dofa (1405), and Donough MacCoilidh, *Erenagh* of Berach, who kept a house of hospitality (1485). According to local tradition, Saint Barry was interred in the doorway of Teach Dorch.

LIFESTYLES, BEHAVIOR, CUSTOMS AND BELIEFS

The lifestyles, behavior and customs of the citizenry of Kinel Dofa were similar to those in tuaths elsewhere in the region. Hanley, like other chieftains of his class, ruled in the broad tradition of the Brehon

Code that the Celts had brought with them when they colonized the island. Gaelic society was uncompromisingly aristocratic and rigidly stratified. It was part and parcel of the culture to claim that rulers and other important people were related to heroic figures of the past.[79] O'Hanley's pedigree was no exception. Social status was measured on the basis of wealth, and wealth meant possessions in land, in clients/vassals and in cattle herds. But ownership of land in Gaelic Ireland wasn't altogether clear. In theory, the land of Kinel Dofa would have belonged to the people; in practice it was another matter.

O'Hanley's longport or stronghold was on a hillside in the townland of Lavagh at the northwestern end of Kilglass parish, a short distance from the spot where the Kilglass lakes empty into Lough Boderg. From there he ruled over a number of tributary septs scattered throughout his Kinel Dofa kingdom. When traveling throughout his kingdom, he was more than likely accompanied by his bodyguard of several hand-picked loyal swordsmen whose duty it was to protect him from assassination, often the fate of chieftains and kings during the Gaelic era.

SUBORDINATE SEPTS

Within Kinal Dofa there were several townlands, each administered by a principal family subordinate to O'Hanley. For example, the townland of Ballyfeeny was administered by the Feeny family; Ballykilcline by the Kilcline family; and Gillstown by the Gill family. There were other families, some of whom are mentioned in the following Medieval poem acclaiming the O'Hanleys:

> *Next let me visit the proud chief O'Hanley,*
> *Who, with a voice so warlike, fierce and manly,*
> *Commands the Kinel Dofa; brave MacShanley,*
> *The lion hearted, raven haired O'Branly*
> *The bloody handed, fiery eyed O'Ganley*

> *The stately statured, bright black eyed O'Hanley*
> *With many others, Cranley, Conlh, and Lee —*
> *These range the Glens and lofty hills of Banlie, Ban Sliabh*
> *Revere Saint Berach and support O'Hanley,*
> *The heir of Dofa and enemy of Stanley.*[80]

The loyalty and acclaim given to O'Hanley by his tributary septs, as recited in the preceding poem, was not always evident among O'Hanley family members themselves. Family feuds, often leading to internecine warfare and killings, seem to have preoccupied much of their lives. The *Annals*[81] record that Maghnus O'hAinlige, chieftain of Kinel Dofa, was slain by the son of his father's brother in 1297. Ivor O'Hanley, heir to the chieftainship of Kinel Dofa, was slain by his own tribe in 1383. Loughlin Oge O'Hanley, Chief of Kinel Dofa, "was treacherously slain in the *crannog* [island residents] of Lough Leise by the son of Murrough, son of Gilla-na-naev O'Hanley, and two other family members (1452)." In his place, Rory Boy (the son of Gilla na naev) was elected chieftain and thereupon hanged the "three family stewards of his own people who had acted treacherously against Loughlin." Thirty years later, in 1482, Loughlin Oge O'Hanley's son Dermot, heir to the chieftainship of Kinel Dofa, was treacherously slain by his kinsmen "in violation of the relics of Connacht and the guarantees of some of its chieftains."

The fifteenth century was also a time of hardship throughout the countryside. The *Annals* describe several catastrophic events: severe frost lasting from November 1434 until February of the following year; great drought in which there was "living fire in the ground;" famine, where people were "forced to eat food unfit to be mentioned;" terrible plagues that wiped out many people; an earthquake in the Oxx Mountains "that killed a hundred people;" and hungry wolves roaming the rural areas devouring people. The inhabitants of Kinel Dofa, like those in the rest of the country, would have endured great suffering.

KILGLASS: FROM BISHOPRIC TO PARISH

In early Christian Ireland, Kilglass was a bishopric or deanery known as Tir hAanlighe (translated means Country of the O'Hanleys), with its own bishop provided by O'Hanley, of course. Following the reorganization of the Irish Church, mandated by the Synod of Kells in 1152, Kilglass became one of five such bishoprics or deaneries merged into one diocese, thereafter the Diocese of Elphin. In 1306, Kilglass was referred to as the "parish of Kilglass" for papal taxation purposes. In 1396, Thomas Barrett (bishop of Elphin at the time) described it as "Kilglass Saint Mary's." A 1405 papal letter to Dr. O'Grady, Bishop of Elphin, referred to it as "Saint Mary's Kilglass."

In those days, the parish church is thought to have been in the northeastern corner of Kilglass graveyard. Finbar O'Mailumayn was appointed pastor of the parish in 1401. He died six years later and was succeeded by Alan Mescallagi. Mescallagi served the parish for less than a year and was succeeded by Florence O'Maelymnayn, who served as pastor until 1411. O'Maelymnayn, in turn, was succeeded by John MacEolich who was referred to in records as "parish priest of Saint Mary's Kilglass." The next recorded appointment (forty-three years later in 1454) was Thomas MacBrayn who was previously a Canon at Clontusket. Dermit MacOncagaid apparently was the last recorded appointment for Kilglass in the pre-Reformation period. He was appointed in 1455 and it is not known how long he served the parish.

Only once, in the next 350 years, was a Roman Catholic priest identified with the parish. He was a Father Terence Neary who was appointed in 1711. According to the Report on the State of Popery for the Diocese of Elphin in 1731, only one mass house existed in Kilglass at the time. The first Catholic church built in post-penal times was erected between 1760–1770. According to popular belief, Protestant services (following the Reformation) were conducted for a number of years in old Saint Mary's Catholic church next to Kilglass graveyard, which had been confiscated. In the early 1800s, Anglican churches were built in Rooskey (1813) and Ruane (1825).

Changing Winds

The sixteenth century brought on new challenges as England moved to tighten its grip on Connacht, long regarded as an isolated lawless area of unconstrained Gaelic chieftains. Henry VIII assumed the English throne and the Protestant Reformation was set in motion. A new phase in Anglo-Irish strife began with religious persecution and Church property confiscation. The first evidence that the Reformation had reached Kinel Dofa was in 1619 when Rev. Daniel O'Farrell was appointed Protestant minister for Ruskey. Fifteen years later, in 1634, Rev. John Nairn was appointed to administer Kilglass, Bumblin and Lisonuffy. Over the next two and a half centuries, a succession of Protestant ministers served the area. The Reformation, followed by the breakup of the old Gaelic order, wrought havoc on the already weakened Catholic Church's ecclesiastical infrastructure. The Penal Laws of the eighteenth century crushed any infrastructure remaining. It was not until the early 1800s that the Catholic Church began to bounce back with the appointment of Father Brian McDermott to Kilglass.

Anarchy Everywhere

If there were social stigmas in Gaelic society, tribal conflict was not one of them. Connacht was torn by the feuds and conflicts brought on by the O'Conors and their kinsmen. When not at war with the Anglo-Normans, they were at war among themselves. As O'Conor power declined and their territory diminished, their quarrels increased and they split into separate and rival clans—O'Conor Roe, O'Conor Don and O'Conor Sligo. These rival O'Conor clans, with their tributary septs, carried on constant hostilities against one another leading to a chronic state of anarchy everywhere.

As the O'Hanley sept was tributary to O'Conor Roe, it was very much a part of the hostilities. The *Annals* contain many references where O'Hanleys are entangled in the armed conflict of the times. In 1311, Tiege O'Hanley was slain by Jordan D'Exeter (sheriff of the English colony), but the attack failed at overthrowing the O'Hanleys who maintained their independence for centuries under their own chieftains. The O'Hanleys participated in the battle between O'Conor Roe and O'Conor Don at Creag in 1396. Among those reported killed were: John O'Teige, the son of John O'Hanley; Con MacBranan, chief of Corca Eachlinn; and Rory MacDermot, lord of Moylurg. Teige MacRannall, lord of Conmaicne, led an army into Kinel Dofa in 1482 to take revenge for the O'Hanleys having violated their guarantees. They burned O'Hanley's house and killed Donough before being routed by O'Hanley's kinsmen.

The litany of depredations and killings continued throughout much of the sixteenth century as well. O'Hanley came under attack from MacDermot of Moylurg, whose predatory intrusions into neighboring territories, including Kinel Dofa, resulted in much plundering and extraction of tribute.

The constant feuding and incessant hostilities among the tribal chiefs of Medieval Ireland ultimately led to great suffering for the inhabitants and, in the end, the ruin of their ancient culture. In 1583 under Queen Elizabeth I, chieftains (Hanley among them) were compelled to surrender their Brehon titles and their possessions to the English Crown. In return, they received re-grants whereby their estates would be passed on to their heirs according to English law instead of being gavelled according to the Brehon law and custom. Charles O'Conor Roe, whose tributary septs included O'Hanley, surrendered the style and kingship of the O'Conor Roe and accepted a re-grant of his territory, which was formed into the barony of Roscommon.

A census taken in 1659 shows the parish of Kilglass as having twenty-three townlands with 208 inhabitants. The low population count, obviously, was from the direct effects of the Cromwellian war. The famine that followed and resultant epidemic are believed to have reduced the population of Connacht by up to thirty percent. Among the Tituladoes, or principal families shown, was one Dermot Hanley, Gent.

HANLEY DIASPORA

Hanleys were among the Wild Geese that fled to the Continent over the centuries. Tadhg Ballagh O'hAinlidhe was among those killed in 1585 when King Phillip of Spain captured Antwerp from the Flemish and Saxons. O'Hanleys who served in the Spanish Netherlands were Don Dionisio Alferez Hannli (1661) and Don Maurisco Hanley (1663).[82]

The Hanleys were dispossessed of much of their lands at the same time as O'Conor Roe ancestral lands were confiscated in the Cromwellian conquest. In 1695, thirty thousand acres (including much of Kinel Dofa) were endowed upon Maurice Mahon in recognition for his service in the Williamite War. The Anglo-Irish landlord had come to replace the chieftain as overlord in the community and the tuath ceased to exist as a political entity. Leading families, Hanley among them, became tenants on their former lands. Charles O'Conor was the last of the O'Conors Roe. He immigrated to the Continent where he died as Governor of Civita Vecchia in the Papal States.

O'DONOVAN ON JOURNEYING THROUGH KILGLASS (1830)[83]

In 1837, John O'Donovan wrote of his travels through the former O'Hanley country. "Yesterday I traversed the parish of Kilglass, which is proverbial in this part of the country for its wickedness. Fear for my safety among the Hanleys and other Lees here mentioned, I employed a car and got Mr. Kelly, of Strokestown, to come with me." He describes how he and his driver traveled through Bumlin and Kiltrustan, past the house of Thomas Charles MacDermott of Toberpatrick, past Gillstown to a steep hill and a very bad road (possibly Tully Hill) over which they experienced some difficulty with the jaunting car. They then traveled on past Lough Lagan, which he pointed out "nearly insulated the county of Kilglass," and how he was struck with the prevalence of black hair in the district. "Hair black as a raven's," he called it, while pondering if these people were, in fact, the descendants of the Firbolgs of Baghna. "It is very probable they are," he wrote, "for a similar process is now going on with regard to the names of the Gaels being assimilated to those of their conquerors, as in Slieve Baan, Quilly to Cox, MacShane to Johnson, O'Braochain to Brougham."

Traveling in a northwest direction through the parish to the foot of Mullaghmaccormac Hill, O'Donovan and his driver met a "respectable-looking" old man named MacShane about whom Kelly whispered, "knows more about Kilglass than any man now living." MacShane greeted them warmly, suggesting to Kelly that he not go any further as the road was too steep and in bad shape. Thereupon, he proceeded to take O'Donovan on foot to the summit of Mullaghmaccormack, where he showed him the panorama that the summit commanded and the various points of interest. Far off in the distance to the west he pointed to Croagh Patrick; to the north and northeast he showed him Slieve Goabach, Slieve-na-ierin and Slieve Russell; to the east he pointed to Brose Hill (Sliabh Bruis) in Cavan and Slieve Cairbre in Longford; and in the southward direction the Four-Mile-House and the top of Slievebawn.

At much closer range, MacShane pointed out the extensive bogs of Termonbarry and the site of Saint Barry's Monastery, just west of the River Shannon, and the constellation of lakes just west of them that divided Kinel Dofa from Tir-Briuin-na-Sionna. MacShane then walked O'Donovan to Cara-na-dTuath Bridge that, he informed them, was built in the year 1741 under the supervision of James Lawder of Kilmore and Richard Nugent of Miltown.

Pleased with all the information MacShane was feeding him, O'Donovan offered to get him a "glass of grog in the Shebeen house," which he declined because he could not drink whiskey since drunk, one night, he had broken a man's collar bone with a loaded whip and was awaiting his trial. "But I can take some at home," he said, "and we'll mix it with milk." They headed to his place where he drank his own very freely. Then, according to O'Donovan, he swore by Saint Barry's crosier and by other far more sacred things that his guests should join him in a drink. When they declined, he pointed to a long pitchfork, a blunderbuss and his two bulldogs to convince them that he was not one to meddle with. "I would have given three shillings at the time to get out of his clutches, but finding that I was in the county of Kilglass I thought it better to let him get his own way," wrote O'Donovan.

O'Donovan, more interested in discussing Saint Barry and his crosier, recorded what MacShane told: "When Barry was blessing this country and the Hanleys (and they are not a bit too blessed now—Tady Hanly of Clooncullaun, an honest, upright man, says that the Hanleys of Lavagh were always a contentious people, fond of law and wrangling and litigation) there was a Huge serpent, or a large worm, used to infest Slievebawn, and Barry chased it from Kilbarry to the brink of Lough Lagan, where it jumped into the water from him, but he made a thrust of the bachall at it and with the vehemence of the thrust he fell on one knee at the brink of the lough: He pierced the worm through, and the blood gushed from the hole made by the top of the bachall in such copious streams that the whole lake was colored red, and from the spot touched by his left knee when he fell, a clear spring well issued which he (Saint Barry) blessed and which to this day retains his blessing."

"Eight years ago (that is, four years before the cholera morbus began) I was drinking whiskey here, and what do you say, but I was on a sudden attacked with a fit of retching and purging and that was followed by violent cramps. I was afraid of my life and my wife set off for Toberbarry, near the old church in Kilglass, at the brink of Lough Lagan, and myself does not know whether she went through the station or not, but she brought me home a bottle of the water and I drank it, and the vomiting and the purging stopped and I was well the next day."

"Well sir, whatever you like, Barry was a blessed man, and some said he was a Hanly file (i.e., hivile); others contended that he was a Cox (Cock's comb), and for that reason both families used to contend for the Gearr Barry (crosier of Barry's). Hanly saying that Saint Barry left the bachall to his ancestor (whose brother he was) and Cox contending that his ancestor was the successor of Saint Barry of Kilbarry, and that it was to him it was left. They used to have it by turns, but latterly neither of them thought much about it, and they gave it to a poor man of the name of Hurraghroe, who used to kill the worm and the fairies, and to cure the blast, and he himself used to carry it about; but it is said that he lent it to a man about six years ago who sent it to Munster where it is at present. It was not in Slieve Baan these six years." O'Donovan had MacShane's story confirmed by an "intelligent man" named Cox and afterwards found out that the crosier was in the possession of a Mr. Pat Shanley, an attorney in Athlone.

After giving O'Donovan and Kelly a good dinner, MacShane accompanied them as far as "Kilglass town, the capital of the county of that name" where he could get more drink. "He got beer which was as sour as cider, and I resumed the conversations about Barry and the families of Slieve Baan," O'Donovan relates. He asked MacShane if he ever heard of Captain Becket of Kilglass, "that celebrated man who used to shoot the Minister's hens and put his pigeons in pound, having first set them drunk." With that, Kelly whispered to O'Donovan, "If you say anything bad of that man here, you'll never bring your head safe out of Kilglass." MacShane went on to say, "That man was a fool. He got drunk here four years ago, and he was drowned in a lough which was about six inches deep."

MacShane brought O'Donovan outside to show him where the Great Glaisne (Becket) was drowned in Lough Lagan, lamenting that he had swam all the lakes in Ireland before he visited Kilglass. "It was prophesied that he would be drowned in some lake, and so he was; he couldn't escape it. He was buried where the churchyard of Kilglass is now, and the old people used to say that he was so big as to reach from one of the graveyards to the other. And still he was drowned in Lough Lagan...." With that O'Donovan and Kelly bid farewell to MacShane.

On their return trip, O'Donovan tells of meeting the "Firbolgs" staggering home from the market. He ends the story of his trip into Hanley country with some lines from the Bard of Ruadh:

> *Of all the parishes (countries) in which the mass*
> *Is read and sung; of all in which the glass*
> *Is drank and broken (smashed), in which each lad and lass*
> *Can swear and swill, and many of them—alas!*
> *In Erin's Isle, are wicked; none surpass*
> *That Hanly's cursed country of Kilglass.*

11

The Three Tuaths—Corca Eachlinn

Corca Eachlinn, the second of the Three Tuaths, was also a petty kingdom and a part of a Gaelic enclave in eastern Connacht. The name Corca Eachlinn, meaning the "Race of Eachlinn," suggests that the area once belonged to a sept, or a leader of a sept, by the name of Eachlinn. No light has been shed on who Eachlinn was. He was probably an ancestor of one of the early Firbolg tribes that inhabited the area who escaped mention in the history books.

In area, Corca Eachlinn approximated the parishes of Bumlin, Kiltrustan and Cloonfinlough and the western half of Lissonuffy parish. At its northern end the River Owenure separated it from its sister tuath, Tir-Briuin-na-Sionna, ruled by O'Beirne. In earlier times, its northwest corner was west of Elphin at Shankhill where a church known as Senchell Dumaige[84] stood. Today, a graveyard marks the spot. Its northeast corner was located at Bela-na-Grange on the road from Strokestown to Drumsna. This was also the point at which all three Tuaths met. Slievebawn was its eastern boundary, the ridge separating it from Kinal Dofa, ruled by O'Hanley. According to local lore, the boundary was marked in former times by a series of upright stones and crosses. The west face of the mountain belonged to MacBrennan, the east face to O'Hanley.

Over the course of time Corca Eachlinn's territorial boundaries shifted. In ancient times, the area is thought to have extended from Slievebawn in the south to Tirerrill barony (County Sligo) in the north, and this would have included the area that became known as Moylurg. Before O'Mulrooney (Sil Murrey) was given or acquired Moylurg, in which he founded an independent tribe or tuath, the area belonged to McGreevy. McGreevy, according to some sources, is said to have been lord of the Callraighe tribes inhabiting the area from pre-Gael times. The *Annals of Loch Ce* confirms that Niall McGreevy was Lord of Callraighe when he died in 1105. A fourteenth century topographical poem by John O'Dugan, lists several families native to the area before O'Mulrooney set up a kingdom there. MacBrennan or Mulvihill are not among them.

The district around the present-day town of Elphin (a part of Corca Eachlinn when Saint Patrick visited Archdruid Ona at Imleach Ona) later became part of Clann Chathail, the territory of the O'Flanagan sept. But territorial boundary shifts were not all that uncommon in ancient times as power structures changed.

Territorial Chieftains

Corca Eachlinn was ruled by Clan MacBrennan whose ancestry can be traced all the way back to the Archdruid Ona in the fifth century. At one time, Clan O'Mailmichil (O'Mulvihill)[85] is believed to have ruled as co-chief with MacBrennan. They were probably two branches of the one family. By the mid-fourteenth century, however, O'Mulvihill had relocated to the southwestern area of present-day County Leitrim where they were chiefs of an area named Cerballain.

MacBrennan was present at the inauguration of Cathal Crobhderg O'Conor as King of Connacht at Carnfree in 1201. He is referred to as the King's "henchman and chief of his kerne, and the caretaker of his hounds." There was no mention of a roll for O'Mulvihill at the inauguration. Neither is the name mentioned in John O'Dugan's fourteenth century topographical poem from which the following lines, memorializing MacBrennan as the chief of Corca Eachlinn, are taken:[86]

Long live the great and brave MacBranain,
The noble chief of old Corca Achlann,
Who from his frontiers views the Shannon,
Around whom flock the tall Ua Siondain,
The pious Doovhies and the Banans,
The fierce MacIgoes and the Fanans
Until the noble Shannon cease to flow,
Until the old Baghna's Mount shall sink
Below the level of Conacia's rich green plain,
May Ona's heir be ever seen to reign.

One of the earliest mentions of Corca Eachlinn is in the Stokes translation of the *Tripartite of Saint Patrick*, which was written in the seventh century, but was probably based on earlier works contemporary to Patrick's time. Also included is the story of Patrick visiting the territory of Corca Eachlinn to the north of Badgna (the ancient name of Slievebawn) where he met with the Archdruid Ona and his brother Id. The site of their meeting was then known as Imleach Ona. Ona was undoubtedly a prominent personage in his community, as his title archdruid would imply. Unlike the Gaulish druids who were under one head druid with supreme authority, Irish druids lacked such a tradition. P.W. Joyce points out that in Ireland "there were eminent druids in various districts, with the influence usually accorded to eminence."[87]

Patrick needed a piece of land to build a church. Ona had the land, but he demanded gold in exchange for it. Patrick insisted he didn't have the gold and instead offered Ona a piece of God's celestial land (heaven) in exchange for the terrestrial plot on which to build his church. The wizard (as Irish druids were called) became very apprehensive of Patrick's insistence. Ono insisted on payment in gold. Patrick prayed God would find him some gold. His prayers were answered when he went to a nearby hillock where the sod was uprooted by swine. There, he found a stash of gold sufficient to pay Ona for the piece of land.

This magic performed by Patrick greatly impressed Ona for the druids had a reputation of being great magicians in their own right. In old historical tales, battles sometimes were determined not so much by the valor of the combatants as by the magical power of the druids attached to the armies. We are told that they could "raise druidical clouds and mists, and bring down showers of fire and blood; they could drive a man insane or into idiocy by flinging a magic wisp of straw in his face." Jocelin, a monk of Furness in Lancashire who wrote about Saint Patrick in the twelfth century, describes how magicians, evildoers, and soothsayers abounded in Ireland in pre-Christian times.[88] Patrick and his disciples were known to have often prayed for protection against the spells of the druids.

Ona was so impressed that he offered Saint Patrick his own fort to build his church. He renamed the place Ail-Finn: *Ail* (stone) from the stone that was raised out of the well that Patrick dug on the spot; and *Finn* (fair) from the water. Patrick then blessed Ona and said, "your seed will be blessed, and from your seed will spring priests of the Lord and heads of churches worthy to receive my dues and your inheritance."[89] In another version, Patrick also told Ona that neither he nor his progeny would ever be kings.

CHRISTIANITY SUPPLANTS DRUDISM AT ONA'S FORT

According to tradition, Saint Patick built a church on the spot of Ona's fort and appointed Assicus as its first bishop. Little is known of Assicus' successors until the twelfth century. There is vague mention of a school at the spot that "grew in reputation." It was probably a branch of one of the many centers of learning that were an outgrowth of the monastic movement of the sixth century. The secular history of the area in the centuries following Saint Patrick's visit provides little of interest or importance. The *Annals* allude to persons such as Flaithniadh, Mailmichil, Adith, Morough and Branain[90] who may have been chieftains or religious leaders of the area. As in other parts of Ireland, widespread acceptance of Christianity was a gradual process. We are told that after Saint Patrick's death, the druids recovered some of the influence they had lost during his thirty years of preaching, and they crusaded against the spread of the new faith. But some form of religious institution seems to have flourished at the spot where Saint Patrick founded the church (which became known as Elphin) where the Archdruid Ona had once performed druidism to the pagan natives.

According to the annalists, the Augustinian Canons arrived in Elphin in 1140 to replace the earlier monastic order. In 1152, the Synod of Kells merged six religious sees into what became known as the Diocese of Elphin and selected Elphin itself as the seat of the bishopric. Donald O'Duffy (d. 1137) is believed to have been the first bishop of the reorganized diocese. He sponsored the crafting of the beautiful Cross of Cong (now preserved in the National Museum in Dublin) as a place of safekeeping for a portion of the true cross. Many of the early bishops belonged to prominent families such as the O'Conors, MacDermots and the Flanagans. However, from the early thirteenth century (following the arrival of the Anglo-Normans), the King of England insisted on the right to grant permission to elect bishops and to confirm the elected or appointed candidate to office.[91]

In 1450, the Franciscans were designated to run the parish by Bishop Conor O'Mullaly, himself a Franciscan. In 1563, following the Protestant Reformation, their monastery was suppressed and their lands given to a Terance O'Beirne by the newly appointed Protestant bishop, Roland de Burke. In 1588, the friary became the possession of John Lynch (during the Elizabethan persecution of Catholics) who replaced de Burke as bishop. In 1615, friary and lands were granted to Sir John King. Two years later, the friary was demolished and, some thirty years later (during the Cromwellian War), the Franciscans were expelled.

The first schismatic bishop of the diocese was Connacht O'Shield (O Siaghail) who had been chaplain to Manus O'Donnell, chieftain of Tyreconnell. O'Donnell recommended him for the post to Henry VIII, and when the dean and chapter refused to elect him, Henry appointed him on his own authority.[92] However, it was not until the seventeen century that Protestantism succeeded in making any headway in Elphin.

The Cathedral was partly destroyed in 1641, rebuilt in 1757 and again in 1853 when it was extensively refurbished. It ceased to function as a place of worship in 1961 when the seat of the Elphin Anglican See was transferred to Sligo.

CLAN MACBRENNAN

The factual history of the MacBrennans begins in the twelfth century and may be reconstructed from manuscripts such as the *Annals of Lough Ce* (1014–1590), the *Annals of Connacht* (1244–1562), the *Annals of the Four Masters* (to 1607), and the writings of historians like O'Donovan, Sharkey and others. Much of what is told relates to events connected with tribal warfare and hostilities. Inasmuch as Saint Patrick had prophesied to Ona that his descendants would not be kings, none of the MacBrennans ever attained that honor. They were, however, trusted sub-chiefs and supporters of the O'Conor kings. As previously mentioned, MacBrennan was the King of Connacht's "henchman and chief of his kerne, and the caretaker of his hounds." The MacBrennans were also described as *erenaghs*[93] of Saint Patrick's church at Elphin. As such, they were responsible for looking after the lands belonging to the church for which they received a stipend. This fact might be considered as a fulfillment of Patrick's other prophesy, "...and from your seed will spring priests of the Lord and heads of churches worthy to receive my dues and your inheritance."

MacBrennan Tribal Encounters

The MacBrennans were no exception to the chronic state of anarchy that pervaded the social and political mainstream of the age. As tributary to the O'Conors Roe, they too were caught up in the constant feuds, raids, battles and killings. The *Annals* contain many references to MacBrennan combat entanglements. One entry (in 1225) describes a raiding party that came upon Echmarcach MacBrennan and a few of his followers in the middle of an oak wood where he was surrounded by his women folk and cattle, and how he fought with uncommon valor until he was killed. In 1295, the O'Kellys killed Conn MacBrennan, chief of the name. In the same year MacBrennan's successor, Tomaltach MacBrennan, was killed by the O'Conallains. In turn, Tomalach's successor, Echmarcach, died of battle wounds in 1319. Uilliam MacBrennan's son, Brian, was killed in 1390. In 1396, Diarmaid O'Conor Roe killed another chief of the name, Conn, at Creaga.

Throughout the fifteenth century, a MacBrennan was as likely to be killed by one of his own kinsmen as by his neighbors. Conn MacBrennan wanted the chieftainship so badly that he killed one of his kinsman in 1401 and another in 1411 to get it. An entry for 1416 records Cormac Dub MacBrennan being killed by other MacBrennans. In 1422, there is the gruesome account of Aireachtach MacBrennan's five sons being killed in one day by the descendants of Conchobar MacBrennan and Echmarcach MacBrennan. It describes how Sean and Bomnal Buide MacBrennan were the first to be killed, at a place called Lis Ferban, followed by Murchad Buide and Brian Dubsuilech at a place called Cell Lacocc. The irony of this killing is that the attackers set fire to the church, forcing the pair into the open rather than killing them inside, which apparently was prohibited. The last to be killed was Eogan Caech at Achad-Beoil-na-Muilled by the sons of Echmarcach MacBrennan, who "came northwards to do the killing, though they did not dare to approach him until they killed him with arrows."

In 1469, another gruesome tale describes an incident in which Tadc, son of Magnus (son of Seoan MacBrennan who was chief of the name), was treacherously killed by his brother Domnall (son of Cormac) and his brother's sons a week after Michaelmas. In 1471 at Lissonuffy, in violation of the oaths and guarantees of the kings and chieftains of Sil Murray, Domnall (son of Cormac, son of Magnus MacBrennan) was treacherously killed by Conn (son of Tadc MacBrennan) who had previously submitted to him. Emann (son of Brian, son of Magnus) was killed with him. In 1496, Teige MacBrennan was murdered by his brother and his nephew, Domnall.

THE DECLINE OF THE MACBRENNANS

The feuding and depredations continued into the sixteenth century. In 1526, O'Conor Roe and the sons of Echmarach MacBrennan drove out Hugh MacBrennan (son of Teige). It is believed Hugh was the last chief of the name in Corca Eachlinn. O'Conor Roe is thought to have seized the territory about this time, possibly needing resources to meet his rising military expenses. Throughout Connacht the old Gaelic order was weakening. The incessant warring and the devastation from the horrifying warfare were taking a toll, not only on the warring factions, but the people in general. Divided and weakened, Gaelic Ireland was incapable of withstanding the powerfully disciplined English forces and, predictably, its outmoded fragmented political structures collapsed.

In 1583 under Elizabeth, the Connacht chieftains were compelled to surrender their Brehon titles and possessions to the English Crown; in return they received re-grants. Charles O'Conor Roe, whose tributary septs included MacBrennan, surrendered his holdings and accepted a re-grant of his territory that was formed into the barony of Roscommon.

A century later, confiscation of the O'Conor Roe ancestral lands by the Anglo-Irish Mahon family brought an end to the old Gaelic political structure of Corca Eachlinn (and part of neighboring Kinel Dofa). A new era had arrived, though it was not necessarily an improvement on what it had replaced. Ironically, those it was designed to deliver from the bondage of the Gaelic tribal lords, the peasants, were the very ones that were enslaved by the new landlord class.

According to the *Tithe Applotment Survey* (1823–1838), there were several branches of the MacBrennan family still inhabiting Lissonuffy parish in 1836. O'Donovan, touring the area in 1837, describes a Hubert Brannan living on a fifty-six acre remnant of the estate of his ancestors in the townland of Belmount. A variation of the name MacBrennan (now more commonly Brennan) is still prevalent in what was formerly Corca Eachlinn.

O'Duffy and Carlos were among other family names associated with Corca Eachlinn. John O'Donovan found the ruins of "a very curious church," which he was told was from the sixth century where it was erected on the site of an ancient fort belonging to O'Duffy. The area he was referring to was Lissonuffy, or the Fort of the O'Duffys. However, O'Donovan questioned the accuracy of the story, stating that the name O'Duffy was not in existence in the sixth century, and the church, which was of Gothic style, couldn't have been erected there earlier than the twelfth century. He concluded that the O'Duffys were the ancient *erenachs* of the church who, according to tradition, came west from County Louth at an early date and settled the area.[94]

Much has been recorded about the O'Duffys who were regarded as one of Connacht's eminent ecclesiastical families in medieval times. Brendan O'Duffy (d. 1136) and Flanagan O'Duffy (d. 1168) are recorded as having been bishops of Elphin. Flanagan, however, is described in the *Annals* as "of Sil Murray" rather than "of Elphin" because at the time Ardcarne was the seat of the bishopric, so designated in 1111. Forty years later, the Synod of Kells (1152) selected Elphin in preference to Ardcarne. Maurice O'Duffy (d. 1174) was Abbot of Boyle when the Abbey was moved there in 1161. In 1175,

King Rory O'Conor selected Archbishop O'Duffy of Tuam as his ambassador to the Court of Henry II.

12

The Three Tuaths—Tir Briuin

Tir-Briuin (or Tir-Briuin-na-Sionna), the most northerly of the Tri Tuaths, was an area of thirty to thirty-five square miles in northeastern County Roscommon, approximating the parishes of Aughrim, Kilmore and Clooncraft. It was separated from its sister tuaths: Kinel Dofa by a chain of lakes stretching from Carnadoe to Muckanagh, collectively called the Kilglass Lakes; from Corca Eachlinn by the River Owen Oor; and in its northern and eastern limits by the River Shannon and the picturesque Lough Boderg. John O'Donovan, in his travels around Connacht in 1837, described the area as very beautiful, interspersed with lakes and marshes, and having a commanding view of the blue range of Slieve-in-Ierin which, he felt, enhanced the sublimity of the scenery. "I am not surprised," he writes, "that the O'Beirnes made such a mighty exertion to wrest it from the O'Monaghans, for it is a district worth fighting for." O'Monaghan controlled Tir Briuin before it was seized by O'Beirne sometime in the latter half of the thirteenth century.[95]

THE EARLY HISTORY

The history of Tir-Briuin reaches back to at least the fifth century. The *Tripartite Life of Saint Patrick* mentions that Saint Patrick crossed the River Shannon, where the village of Drumsna now stands, and went to nearby Moyglass (Kilmore) where the locals received him with open arms. They presented him with a piece of land on which he laid the foundation of a church, afterwards named Cill-Mor-Maigh-Glaise or "the great church of the green plain." He named two disciples, Conleng and Ercleng, to carry on his missionary work in the area before proceeding on his journey. In 1232, Con MacGiolla O'Flanagan of Boyle Abbey built the Priory of Saint Mary for the Augustine Canons on the location. Bishop O'Conor of Elphin (1231–1245) consecrated the church, and it was occupied by the Order for several centuries before it was dissolved in 1539.

During the Elizabethan period, the priory and lands were granted to Tyrell O'Farrell and later given to Dr. Edward King, Protestant bishop of Elphin (1611–1639). Over time, the priory fell into decay and in the late eighteenth or early nineteenth century it was demolished. An Anglican church, part of which is still standing, was erected in its place.

Territorial Chieftains

A celebrated warrior named Mannachan, leader of a Firbolg tribe Ui Manachain,[96] emerged as the territorial chieftain of Tir-Briuin in the ninth century. He is first mentioned by the annalists in reference to an altercation in 866 between Conor, son of King Tadgh Mor of Connacht[97] and Flam, son of Conaig, Lord of Breagh.[98] O'Dugan describes the Connachtmen's victory and Mannachan's fierce bravery in slaying Flam, whose severed head he presented to Conor.[99] In reward for his services, Mannachan was given the lordship over Tir-Briuin.

It was from Mannachan that Ui Manachain (O'Monaghan) took its name, and its sept history can be reconstructed from the *Annals* and similar works on the era. Much of the information, however, is about feats and deaths of chieftains and tribal feuds and altercations. There are references describing O'Monaghan as "Lord of Ui-Briuin" during the twelfth and thirteenth centuries. There are also references recounting the slayings of Donn O'Monaghan, *Toisach* (chieftain) of Tir-Briuin in 1145, and Muredach O'Monaghan, lord of Tir-Briuin, at the Battle of Ardee in 1159. An entry for 1196 records the death of Ignatius O'Monaghan who is described as lord of Tir-Briuin. The last reference to an O'Monaghan, as chieftain of the territory, is an entry in the *Annals of Connacht* for 1287 mentioning the death of Gilla-of-the-Horses O'Monaghan, referring to him as "king of the Tri Tuatha."

O'Monaghan, however, was not among the dynasts attending the inauguration of Cathal Crobhderg as King of Connacht eighty-six years earlier in 1201, notwithstanding his position as lord of Tir Briuin. Instead, it was O'Beirne who was present as chief of the territory, and it was O'Beirne who was listed among the privileged stewards of the King's household. However, the O'Monaghans managed to hold onto substantial prestige, notwithstanding the rising importance of O'Beirne. References in the *Annals*[100] give credence to this: Gillachrist O'Managhan died in Rome in 1216; Lochlin O'Monaghan, "tigerna" Ui-Briuin-na-Sionna, slain in 1227; Maelsechlainn O'Monaghan killed by his own brethren in 1230; and the three sons of Donn O'Monaghan slain by Donnahada, son of Muirchertach at Termon Caelain in 1232.

O'MONAGHANS OUSTED BY O'BEIRNES

The first reference to a feud between the O'Monaghans and O'Beirnes is noted for 1268. The entry records that Domhnal, son of Tadgh O'Monaghan, and ten of his people were slain by Tadgh O'Flanagan and Gilla Christ O'Beirne. This could well have been the decisive episode in an otherwise protracted struggle that finally ousted the O'Monaghans from Tir-Briuin. There are no further references to the O'Monaghans in the *Annals*, except for Gilla-na-nEch O'Monaghan's obituary in 1287. One could safely assume that it was a leadership struggle that may have gone on for most of the thirteenth century. This struggle appears to have been solely between the two families. There is no hint that the O'Hanleys or the MacBrennans from the neighboring tuaths were drawn into the conflict. Probably, they had their own struggles to contend with. Only the O'Flannagans are mentioned as having sided with the O'Beirnes. An old poem, here in literal translation, gives mention to the hostilities:[101]

> *The great O'Beirnes, that bright brave band*
> *Got o'er the O'Monaghans chief command*
> *And since they came their lands they hold*
> *By fights, frays, threats and courage bold.*

After the O'Beirnes assumed the lordship of Tir-Briuin, they made their headquarters at Mura-na-Manachain, a hilltop fort northeast of Elphin that they obviously acquired as part of the spoils when they ousted the O'Monaghans. They renamed it Lios-a-Duirn (Lissadorn), meaning Fort-of-the-Fist, preserving a myth that O'Beirne killed O'Monaghan there with a blow of his fist. The O'Beirnes remained there until the mid-1500s when an Elisabethan adventurer named Crofton ousted them and took over their lands. Thereafter, their headquarters is identified as Dangan Castle, located close to the Priory of Saint Mary in Kilmore. The castle (said to have been built by an O'Brannan) is thought to have come into the possession of the O'Beirnes through marriage.

O'Beirne ruled Tir-Briuin for more than three centuries. He was constitutional chieftain and carried on his role as ruler in accordance with proscribed tuath customs. O'Beirne was, according to the Brehon laws, the leader in war and governor in peace, but at the same time he and the other families of the tuath were mutually dependent upon each other. He owed allegiance to O'Conor, but he did not necessarily side with his over-king in every military engagement.

The *Annals* record that a Donnachad O'Birn, chieftain of Tir-Briuin, was the principal ally of Conor MacDermot of Moylurg against Turlough O'Conor in a battle near Elphin in 1342, where the casualties on O'Conor's side were heavy. One account tells of Turlough being chased in disgraceful retreat into a church at Elphin, where he was set upon by Cathal O'Beirne who gave him a lash across the head, calling him a hog to which the king angrily retorted, "May it bring no good to the swineherd."

Much of O'Beirne's influence as lord of Tir-Briuin was during a period of relentless warfare among the Gaelic chieftains, and when it came to fighting, the O'Beirnes were not above reproach. The *Annals* relate how, in 1375, unnamed assailants attacked Cormac O'Birn and many were killed including Donough O'Birn. Thadeus O'Birn was thrown in jail in 1382 because he and three others conspired to depose his overlord, Roderick O'Conor. In 1407, an O'Conor attacked and captured O'Beirne's Castle at Dangan, no doubt in reprisal for earlier assaults from the O'Beirnes.

The O'Beirnes appear to have become more rapacious in the 1400s, taking to cattle raiding, plundering of property and fighting among themselves. In 1451, three sons of Maelschlainn O'Beirne—Teige, William and Donogh—were killed by, among others, sons of his brothers, Cormac and Brian. During the long and severe winter of 1465, Maelschlainn (who was chief at the time) and a son known as Gilla Dub were killed and burned by Maelschlainn's brothers and kinsmen. A few days later, the same assailants killed another son, Cairpre. Cairpre had attacked them at a place called Berna Bailb and was killed with one severe arrow-wound by Muirchertach O'Birn.[102] Another son, Rosa, was killed in a skirmish the following year.

The casualties continued to mount into the sixteenth century as O'Beirnes fought no less among themselves as with their neighbors. A chieftainship succession dispute in 1527 added to the family's woes. Tadc and Maelschlainn (sons of former Chieftain Cairbre O'Birn) seized the chieftainship over the heads of the senior branch of the family (the descendants of Cormac) after Chieftain Domnall died. Tadc became chieftain and Maelschlainn became *tanist* (heir apparent). Maelschlainn, described as Rory MacDermot's[103] foster-brother and regarded as a widely respected scholar, was killed in 1535 by the sons of Cathal-mac-Rory-Og MacDermot at Mullaghnashee. Although those who committed the crime were banished from Moylurg, the

O'Beirnes took revenge by killing Conor Garbh MacDermot (son of Cathal-mc-Rory-Og) the following year. Two years later in 1538, the *Annals* record how an O'Birn aided the O'Conor Don in resolving a dispute between warring branches of the MacDermots.

The litany of hostilities and killings continued throughout much of the sixteenth century, further weakening the already shattered tribal kingdoms, including Tir Briuin. Divided and weakened, the O'Beirnes were incapable of holding on to their ancient lands and, predictably, they collapsed from the onslaught of the Tudor re-conquest of Ireland.

Decline in Status

The O'Beirne's decline as lords of Tir-Briuin actually began during the reign of Elizabeth I in the mid-sixteenth century. In 1585, the Compossicion of Connacht was introduced as a means to supplant the Gaelic Brehon Code with the English legal and administrative system, believing it would diminish the endless warfare and hostility that the Gaelic kings and chieftains resorted to for settling their disputes. An Elizabethan adventurer named Crofton took over Lissadorn and its land.

The O'Beirnes retreated to Dangan Castle near the village of Kilmore. In 1585, Carbrye O'Beirne (then chief of his name) signed an indenture relinquishing Dangan Castle and most of the 4,200 acres he had under his control to the English Crown. In return, he was permitted the exclusive use of the land thereafter as a tenant of the Crown. The remainder of the lands went to a Donagh O'Beirne of Dowen under the same terms. However, in the early 1600s, the castle and lands were granted to Edward King of Charlestown who was subsequently appointed the Protestant Bishop of Elphin (1611–1639). O'Beirne was permitted to remain in the Castle for a nominal rent, believed to have been a compromise worked out after the good bishop realized it would have been a difficult engagement to have him evicted. The castle had fallen into ruin by the time Bishop King took possession. It was originally built in the thirteenth century and rebuilt about 1453 after it was destroyed by fire. Sources have described it as an "impressive impregnable fortress of four towers, each containing four balustraria, and connected by walls supported by a strong stone balluim."

Early in the 1600s, title to land became a cause of great concern for Gaelic families such as the O'Beirnes. Six of Ulster's counties had been planted by Scots and English settlers, as had neighboring County Leitrim. Roscommon looked vulnerable. Already, vast tracts had passed into the possession of settlers. For instance, in 1641, thirty-eight of forty transactions that involved O'Beirnes were in one direction: from them to persons with English or Anglo-Norman names. Cromwell arrived in Ireland in 1649 and, after a campaign of unprecedented ferocity, succeeded in crushing all organized opposition.

Following the surrender of Connacht forces (1662), an Act of Parliament (1663) designated Roscommon as one of the areas where those families (Gaelic and old Norman stock) from the other three provinces, whose lands had been confiscated, were transplanted. "To Hell or to Connacht" became the choice, meaning that the western province was synonymous with hell. The Tri Tuaths (redesignated the barony of Ballintober North) were targeted as a transportation destination for Irish widows and orphans of English extraction. The O'Beirnes were not transplanted; they were already in Connacht.

Despite the reality of the social and economic upheavals of the Cromwellian War and their diminished status, the O'Beirnes were listed as landholders under seven versions of the name ten years later. Ten years later, the surname was relatively numerous in the district they had once controlled.[104]

Further confiscation of lands occurred after the Williamite Wars (1690s). The O'Beirnes are believed to have been among the Irish officers of the defeated Jacobite army who were permitted to leave Ireland for the Continent. There is little historical reference to the O'Beirne name from then until the late 1700s when Colonel Andrew

O'Beirne of Dangan House, described as the Chieftain, lost his lands allegedly due to his involvement with the revolutionary United Irishmen. While there is no direct evidence that he participated in any of the revolutionary activities of that time, it is significant, as pointed out by Dr. Bryan Beirne,[105] that one of the primary conflicts in that part of Ireland was in the region of Dangan where in 1793, about 3,600 armed defenders from Kilmore, Aughrim and Kilglass parishes assembled at Kilmore and marched north to take over Drumsna and its bridge over the Shannon. They were met and defeated by a well-led, disciplined company of the Derry Militia in what became known as "The Fight at Drumsna Bridge."

Andrew O'Beirne's estates and property were divided among the descendants of earlier interlopers in the area. Among them were King, Lawder, Kelly, French (who evidently got Dangan House) and Greville. The O'Beirnes were allowed to remain in Dangan House as renters until the 1850s.

OTHER TIR BRIUIN SEPTS

There were, of course, other septs in Tir-Briuin, many of whom were tributary to O'Beirne. As was the circumstance with other lesser-known septs throughout the tuaths of Gaelic Ireland, little is told about the families that inhabited O'Beirne's realm.

John O'Donovan, who visited the area in 1837, described visiting an old graveyard called Aughrim, and the ruins of a small building called Beech Abbey (anciently known as Kill Ceanuran) and not being able to find "a curious tombstone or monument in the graveyard worth mentioning." However, he was impressed with its pleasing view of Culnahinse Lough, the steeple of Elphin Cathedral and the lovely countryside of Tir Briuin. He noted that the *Four Masters* used the Gaelic term *Eachdhruim* for Aughrim, calling the church Eachdhruin Mac-n-Aodha, meaning the Aughrim of MacKee or MacHugh, the name of a family who were the ancient *erenachs* in the area.

One distinguished family inhabiting Tir-Briuin was O'Maolchonaire (O'Mulconroy), a family of hereditary men of letters who were poets and scribes to the O'Conors and other illustrious Connacht families. The family seat was on Lough Cloonahee, three miles northeast of Elphin. Two of the better-known members of the family, brothers Fearfasa and Muiris, assisted Michael and Conaire O'Cleary in compiling the *Annals of the Kingdom of Ireland* (later renamed the *Annals of the Four Masters*) between 1632 and 1636. Two other family members were distinguished ecclesiastics: Thomas, Archbishop of Tuam (d. 1266) and Florence (Conroy) who died in 1629. Another O'Mulconroy was a Franciscan priest and grammarian who wrote a "grammatical" tract in manuscript on the subject of prosody in Madrid in 1659. Yet another, Sir John Conroy, was created a Knight Commander of Hanover by King George IV and received many other distinguished honors for his long and faithful services to the Duke and Duchess of Kent and to Princess Victoria (later Queen Victoria) who later made him a baron.

The O'Mulconroys resided at Cloonahee from the twelfth century until 1853 when their property passed out of the family. The family was deprived of their lands during the seventeenth century, but retrieved most of it when they changed to the Protestant faith and changed their name to Conroy. In the mid-nineteenth century, the family's fortunes diminished and the estate at Cloonahee was sold to a man named John Hague, who a short time thereafter sold it to a gentleman by the name of Higgins. In 1927, a solicitor named Patrick Callery (who had been born in nearby Coolmeen) purchased Cloonahee House and adjoining land. The present owner is Patrick's son, James Callery, a prominent local businessman. There were other branches of the Conroy family who owned considerable property in the immediate locality of Cloonahee. Few traces of those families are now to be found.

13

Conquest and the Anglo-Irish Ascendancy Era

Throughout the eighteenth century, the Anglo-Irish landed class held a virtual monopoly on political, economic and religious power in Ireland.

For two hundred years, from the end of the Williamite War in the late 1600s to the arrival of real democracy in the 1880s, Ireland was ruled by an oligarchy of landed Anglo-Irish Ascendancy families. It was made up mostly of descendants of people of English origin who had settled in Ireland from the sixteenth century onward, usually after receiving grants of land for military or other services to the British Crown. Their religious affiliation was Protestant, limited to the Anglican faith; other Protestant creeds, such as Presbyterians, were not included.

Anglo-Irish Ascendancy families were a narrow social and political elite, an ethnic group to which only the higher echelons of the Anglo-Irish belonged. There were many English settlers in Ireland who were socially not part of the Anglo-Irish Ascendancy. By the same token, many families not of English origin became part of the Anglo-Irish establishment (Anglo-Norman families like the FitzGeralds, and Gaelic families such as the Quins of Adare and the O'Haras of Lehney) upon conforming to the Anglican religion. Affiliation in the Anglican Church and the right family connections held the key to membership in this elite league, and only the membership profited from its oligarchy circle.

Throughout the eighteenth century, the Anglo-Irish Ascendancy held a virtual monopoly on political, economic and religious power in Ireland, which they had seized in the aftermath of the Williamite War of 1689–1691. It was the culmination of more than a century of struggle, which began when Henry VIII attempted to bring together the autonomous Gaelic kingdoms under the umbrella of his newly created Kingdom of Ireland and extend English law and government to the whole island. It was at this crucial juncture of political events that the religious discussion entered English-Irish relations. Henry broke with Rome, not out of doctrinal differences but over the question of divorcing his first wife, Catherine of Aragon. The English Parliament moved to recognize him as "supreme head of the English Church," and the spiritual authority in England, which had belonged to the papacy, was afterward invested in the English monarch.

Henry moved quickly to overthrow "native rule," and to replace papal with royal authority in the Irish Church as well. In 1536, he convened the Irish Parliament to enact Reformation statutes and make the Dublin administration more pro-English by increasing the number of key positions filled by English-born persons. The following year, a "Reformation Parliament" met and enacted laws disavowing papal authority and requiring that officeholders take an oath acknowledging the supremacy of Henry, who assumed the title of "King of Ireland." Henry then appointed George Browne as the Protestant Archbishop of Dublin and assigned him the unpopular task of reforming the Irish Church.

Henry's successors, Edward VI and Mary Tudor, took a more aggressive approach toward the Gaelic lords, demanding the forfeiture of lands in Counties Laois and Offaly, accompanied by the establishment of new military garrisons. In 1558, along came Elizabeth I who immediately embarked on a campaign of militant pursuit against hostile Gaelic chieftains. She successfully put down rebellions by the Desmonds in Munster and confiscated their lands. She was less successful against the Ulster O'Neill and O'Donnell chieftains who continued to hold out successfully until they were finally defeated at Kinsale in 1602, firmly establishing English hold over much of Gaelic Ireland.

Confiscation and Plantation

After Kinsale Elizabeth's successor, James I, undertook the plantation of confiscated Ulster lands with Scottish and English settlers. Outside Ulster, Gaelic lords still owned much of the richest land, but their representation in the Dublin parliament had dipped to that of minority status. Rivalry intensified between the prominent Gaelic families and the newer landlords (who were increasing significantly in number) and anti-Catholic sentiment was heightening.

A rebellion by Gaelic/Catholic lords in 1641 attempted to overthrow the predominantly Protestant government in Dublin in place since Henry VIII's time. The reigning monarch, Charles I, issued a proclamation calling on those at war in Ireland to surrender. This was not enough to satisfy the Dublin Protestant government, and its call for revenge and confiscation resulted in the English parliament passing the "Adventurers" bill to encourage investment in the re-conquest of Ireland.[106]

The following year, leading Catholics from Old English and Gaelic families met in Kilkenny and set up a provisional assembly, but were unable to make substantial progress because irreconcilable differences surfaced between the two groups. In Dublin, the chief Protestant stronghold, the regular parliament expelled its forty-one Catholic members. But the events in Ireland in the following years were rewritten as a result of events in England. A civil war erupted. The army moved in and set up a Puritan regime under Cromwell. The king was beheaded.

WAR AND MORE WARS

Following the execution of Charles I, Cromwell invaded Ireland in 1645 with seventy thousand troops, determined to crush the Irish and obliterate the Catholic religion. The war lasted seven years and, when it ended in 1652, Cromwell had succeeded in accomplishing much of what he set out to do. During that period some two-thirds of a million people, nearly a third of Ireland's population of one and a half million, had died from war, disease or famine.

The restoration of the monarchy in 1660 under Charles II brought some relief for Catholic landowners. Some had their estates restored to them if they could prove non-participation in the conflict. Nonetheless, Catholic landowners were a diminishing class as more and more of their ancestral lands slipped into the hands of Protestant English settlers. In 1641 Catholic landowners held about three-fifths of the country's land; twenty-four years later their ownership had slipped to barely over one-fifth.

Charles was succeeded by James II, the first Catholic monarch since Mary Tudor to rule England. While announcing his intention of respecting Protestant rights, James moved to strengthen the role of Catholics in Irish governmental and military affairs. He revoked the charters of the parliamentary boroughs (established earlier by the crown for the benefit of planted Protestant families) and established in their place administrations strongly royalist and generally Catholic. These changes and the appointments of Catholics to key military and government positions caused great trepidation among Ireland's Protestant propertied class. It was the birth of his son in 1688 by his second wife, however, that raised fear in the Protestant classes and sealed his doom. England's Tories invited his son-in-law, William of Orange, to accept the crown. James escaped to France where he took refuge at the court of his cousin Louis XIV.

William was not as well accepted in Ireland as he was in England. The Catholics, still bitter at the Cromwellians, revolted everywhere.

James landed in Ireland the following year and put himself at the head of what had become a predominantly Catholic movement. He reorganized the Irish army, replacing Protestant officers with Catholics. He appointed Catholics to judgeships and to the privy council, and the Protestants were given the same harsh treatment that had been meted out to Catholics during earlier conflicts.

Concerned with what was happening, William led an army into Ireland and after a two and a half years' campaign, defeated James and his Irish supporters. James fled to France; his Irish supporters were given a choice of taking an oath of allegiance to William and returning to their homes, joining the English army, or sailing for France. Most of them opted for exile, thereby relinquishing their lands and titles.

In the aftermath of the Williamite war, Gaelic society collapsed under an onslaught of draconian laws abolishing civil rights and outlawing Catholic worship by the non-conforming[107] Irish who, at the time, constituted seventy-five percent of the population. William's victory left Ireland in the hands of the Anglo-Irish Protestant Ascendancy, largely the descendants of Tudor and Stuart families who had settled in Ireland over the previous century.

To many historians, King William's victory over King James at the Battle of the Boyne in County Meath in 1689 was the final act in the collapse of Celtic Ireland where Celtic civilization had flourished for more than two millennia. It is true that, from time to time, Celtic Ireland had been in retreat, but it was a slow and stubborn retreat. Until its collapse in the seventeenth century, many features of the Celtic way of life persisted, especially in the western province of Connacht. Historians write that the final collapse only came after the Irish fighting aristocrats had depopulated themselves and were outnumbered by their English invaders. Edmund Curtis' writes of the Irish fighting aristocracy:

> "What was there for these numerous rigdonmas to do, being of noble blood, but to be 'swordsmen' or 'idle men', as the Tudor English called such fighting gentlemen? They took no part in for-

eign wars and seldom or never left their native country. All that was left, if such a one could not be 'king' or 'tanist' in his time, was to seek some new lordship. But most of them perished prematurely in the feuds, the fighting and the forays which they considered to be their raison d'etre, the seniors of their own stock being delighted to diminish the numbers of dangerous rivals by fair means or foul. Still, the numbers of the fighting aristocrats was so great that it took the Tudor sovereigns a whole century before the swordsmen and their world were brought to an end."[108]

William's victory at the Battle of the Boyne in County Meath had consummated the supremacy of the Protestant faith in Ireland, which would last for one hundred and seventy-five years. In 1691, the Treaty of Limerick ended the struggle and ushered in the third great defeat for the Irish Catholic cause in seventeenth century Ireland. The Irish parliament, now entirely Protestant, began work on bolstering the Protestant grip on all walks of life. Both English and Irish Parliaments enacted laws disallowing religious privileges and assurances against further property confiscation granted by King William to Irish Catholics in the Treaty. More than a thousand Catholics had submitted claims for restoration of their lands and while most of these claims were granted, only a small portion of the land—fourteen percent—remained in the hands of Catholic landowners. Most of the Catholic population were now tenants on the land they had previously owned.

THE PENAL LAWS

After the Treaty of Limerick, there was still some of the old Catholic aristocracy standing in the way of total domination. They had to be crushed and to achieve this the Dublin parliament enacted a series of draconian laws aimed at prohibiting Catholics from all direct political influence under the pretense of their disloyalty during the revolution of 1688. These were known as the Penal Laws and under them a Catholic could not acquire land by purchase, inheritance or gift from a Protestant. Catholics were not permitted to teach in schools, serve on juries or as constables, nor could they vote or serve in parliament or the military. Priests were required to register with the authorities, any found not registered were to be branded with a red-hot iron upon the cheek. An amendment added by the Irish Privy Council, substituting castration for branding, was removed when the bill reached Westminster for review. Irish Catholics, traitors in the eyes of the ruling Anglo-Irish Protestant Dublin parliament because they had sided with James, were made to pay for their disloyalty.

For Catholics, the choice to function as normal citizens in their own land was severely curtailed. The options left to them were few—going into exile, giving up their faith, resorting to deception, or taking a downgrade in their social and economic standing. Some did, in fact, become Protestant. Others went through a so-called conversion to the established church in order to secure their property. Most, however, clung to their old faith and were reduced to the level of subsistence farmers.

AN OPPRESSED PEASANTRY

There followed a period of great poverty and hardship among the tenant class. Unresolved grievances (relating to unfair rents, tithes to the Protestant Church of Ireland, and other inequities) often led to violence and disorder as the oppressed peasantry, with nowhere to turn for redress of their problems, resorted to anarchy. Throughout the countryside small local groups formed themselves into secret oath bound societies.

Throughout the century, economic and cultural divisions between landowners and the peasantry continued to widen. Many landlords were living extravagant lifestyles while accumulating debts and financial responsibilities that were passed on to their heirs, making each succeeding generation less prosperous. At the same time the peasant population was increasing at an alarming pace and the great majority, already scarcely surviving, was more and more dependent on the potato for survival. The potato, although not always a reliable crop, enabled large quantities of food to be produced at a minimum cost from a small plot of ground. An acre or so would provide a family of five or six with food for a year. A severe famine in 1740–1741 caused thousands to die of starvation.

Notwithstanding the appalling living conditions of the time, Ireland's population began a rapid rise soon after mid-century. Estimated at three million in 1760, the population had climbed to five million at the end of the 1790s to represent thirty-three per cent of the total population of the British Isles. This phenomenal growth continued well into the nineteenth century. The population had reached over eight million by the 1840s, making Ireland the most densely populated country in Europe. Some attribute Ireland's phenomenal population growth to the bountifulness of two basic essentials, cheaply available in great quantities at the time: an abundance of peat fuel for warmth; and plenty of food, mainly from the nutritional potato, for sustenance.

EMERGENCE OF A GAELIC MIDDLE CLASS

There was a lessening of interference with Catholic worship after the 1720s, and by the middle of the century it had become obvious that the intractable Catholic Irish were beyond hope of conversion to the Established Church. At the same time a middle-class Catholic Irish community of merchants and professionals began to emerge. Excluded from political life, they formed a passive counter culture of which their religion became a central element. They were impatient with a system that kept them outside the political process and they despised the "popery laws" which delegated them to second-class citizenry. Out of this resentment grew the struggle for complete equality and, when that failed to materialize, a struggle for political supremacy emerged.

POLITICAL AND RELIGIOUS REFORM PROGRESS

Movement toward electoral reform in England in the 1780s encouraged movement for change in Ireland. The Catholic Association, founded by Charles O'Conor[109] of Belanagare and others, was the first effort to establish a lobby on behalf of Catholic interests. Towards the end of the 1700s there was modification and relaxation of the "popery act" of 1707. These changes provided some measure of relief as they allowed Catholics to take long leases on land and inherit and bequeath the leases without proscribed restrictions. This was the beginning of the arduous and slow process by which all social and political disabilities were eventually removed over the following half-century.

A bill in 1792 removed disabilities on marriages between Catholics and Protestants and permitted Catholics to be called to the bar. A statute in 1793 gave Catholics the right to vote both in local elections and for members of parliament and opened to them government positions other than the highest civil and military posts. The electorate was restricted, with the franchise firmly based on property ownership. In 1795, attempts to legislate changes that would have admitted Catholics to seats in parliament were resolutely rejected by the British political elite, dashing immediate hopes of full participation by Catholics in the political life of their country.

The 1790s was a decade of crisis for Britain. Abroad, she was at war with France; in Ireland, agrarian unrest against rising tithes and rents was creating disturbances. Reformers, pushing for further constitutional changes, began to organize themselves along military lines and sought help from revolutionary France. They were the United Irishmen, committed to parliamentary reform that, if achieved, would give a vote to every man and establish democratic rule in Ireland.

In many respects the eighteenth century was a period of economic growth and expansion, characterized by a sweeping construction drive of great mansions throughout the countryside for the landed class and the building of private and public buildings in the capital city of Dublin. An agricultural economy, with increasing emphasis on exporting grain, meat and dairy goods, flourished. By the middle of the century Dublin, with a population of more than a 100,000, had become the second city in the British Empire, next to London.

In contrast to all this prosperity, there existed throughout the countryside a peasantry immersed in abject poverty and exploitation by greedy landlords and tithe proctors.

THE ACT OF UNION

In 1798, a revolutionary uprising by the United Irishmen under Theobald Wolfe Tone, seeking to establish an independent Ireland for Irishmen, was quickly crushed by England. The British, recognizing the potential for a serious political problem, set out at once to secure the coalition of both kingdoms. The Act of Union followed in 1801, abolishing the Irish Parliament and substituting in its place Irish representation at Westminster. The Union gave Ireland 100 of the 658 seats in the British House of Commons and 32 seats in a newly expanded House of Lords.

The Union, however, failed to remove the remaining major political disability—the right of Catholics to sit in either House of Parliament. Prime Minister Pitt's effort to deal with this issue at the time of the Union was vetoed by King George III who still saw Catholic emancipation as dangerous and unnecessary. It was a betrayal of those Irish Catholics who had supported the Union. Another twenty-nine years would pass before a massive campaign led by Daniel O'Connell would make Catholic emancipation a reality.

The union of Ireland and England (1801) greatly heightened a coincidental decline in the Irish economy when the removal of tariffs flooded the country with cheap imports and undermined the textile industry. Fourteen years later, the end of the Napoleonic Wars brought widespread economic depression throughout Europe, and a falling demand for Irish agriculture products left many farmers bankrupt.

Calamity struck in the 1840s in the form of the Great Potato Famine. It began in 1845 with the failure of the potato crop, but its worst impact was in 1847. This tragic event led to the death or emigration of more than two million men, women and children, forever altering the course of Irish society. In the decade of the 1840s, the population of Ireland dropped from over eight million to six and one-half million and by the end of the century it had further dropped to four and one half million. It is estimated that from the 1840s to the 1920s, four and three quarter million people left Ireland to make their homes in foreign lands, most of them to North America. The impact on rural Ireland was immense.

THE EMERGENCE OF IRISH NATIONALISM

Irish nationalism began to emerge in the early nineteenth century when the Act of Union (1801) failed to resolve issues of political and social rights for Catholics. It became a distinct issue in 1823 when an Irish Catholic lawyer by the name of Daniel O'Connell and others organized to gain political and social justice for Catholics and to look after the interests of the tenant farmers. The association expanded rapidly throughout the countryside, giving tenant farmers encouragement to flout their landlords' dictates and vote instead for the Association's endorsed candidates. In the 1826 parliamentary elections four candidates supporting Catholic Emancipation were elected despite the law on the books that prevented Catholics from taking their seats in the House of Commons. A by-election in County Clare in 1828 gave O'Connell twice as many votes as the incumbent candidate who had the strong backing of the landlord class.

Westminster was not sure what to do about seating O'Connell. Duly elected by his constituents, it would have been risky to exclude him. Ireland's tenant farmers were seething with economic discontent and were quite capable of starting serious trouble for the landlords. George IV let it be known that it would violate his Coronation Oath if he were to give royal assent to any emancipation bill allowing Catholics to sit in parliament. Prime Minister Wellington, pragmatic enough to see the urgency of yielding on this issue, persuaded the king to go along. Finally, in 1829, the Catholic Relief Bill became law, giving Catholics full political franchise and eligibility for appointment to most offices under the crown.

O'Connell became an instant national hero and went on to found the National Repeal Association in 1841 to secure repeal of the Union. The Tories and the Wigs joined in steadfast opposition to any attempt that would lead to dissolution of the Union. With diminished support, the movement went into decline and finally collapsed following O'Connell's death in 1847.

DEMANDS FOR SELF-GOVERNMENT

The issue of self-government came to the front again in the 1870s. Isaac Butt organized the Irish Party, pledging to obtain a separate legislature for Ireland. It secured more than fifty seats in its first Parliamentary election, lending support for the home-rule bid. Reform measures passed in 1884 and 1885 broadened the householder franchise. Constituency boundaries were redrawn giving urban populations more equitable representation than they had previously enjoyed; for the first time the majority of men enjoyed the vote. Large towns received parliamentary representation proportional to their populations. The franchise extension to the small farmers in the countryside meant that the once dominant position of the landlord class in controlling the House of Commons had ended, but genuine democracy was still in the future.

Charles Stewart Parnell, an ardent nationalist, took over the leadership and succeeded in tabling a measure in the House of Commons calling for a separate parliament in Dublin. In 1886, the first Irish Home Rule Bill, which proposed a parliament for Dublin to legislate

Irish affairs, was submitted to the Westminster Parliament. The Dublin parliament would control the Irish executive and was to have full powers, except on such matters as were reserved for the crown. It was heavily defeated by an alliance of Conservatives and Ulster Protestants with help from Liberal members who broke rank with their party.

Landlords Under Attack

During the 1870s and 1880s a combination of bad harvests, bad weather and falling prices hit Ireland's agriculture economy. The result was misery and starvation to an extent not experienced since the 1840s. Land reform became the rallying cry of the peasant farmers. An explosion of anti-landlord feeling, beginning with the small landholders in County Mayo, spread among the tenant farmers throughout the rest of the country. Mass meetings were held, tenants refused to pay rent, landlords and their agents were subjected to assault, intimidation and social ostracism. In 1879 the disorder expanded into a national protest movement known as the Land League that waged an unrelenting war against landlordism for several years under its leaders Charles Stewart Parnell and Michael Davitt. The Land Leaguers demanded fair rent, a fixed tenure and the ability to sell improvements tenants had made to their property when they disposed of it. The landlords retaliated by evicting recalcitrant tenants in unprecedented numbers.

Times had changed to the disadvantage of the landed Anglo-Irish aristocracy; their arbitrary power had been greatly diminished by the extension of the franchise several decades earlier. Alarmed and overwhelmed by the League's nationwide display of hostile agitation, the Land Act of 1881 was passed which set up a judicial tribunal to examine the gravity of the situation and the possibility of the government making loans available that would enable tenants to purchase their holdings outright. Distressed and demoralized by the land wars, Westminster reluctantly approved buyout provisions, having come to the realization that it could no longer prop up the landed class and their fiefdoms.

In 1885, the Ashborne Act made five million pounds available for land buyouts and five years later this amount was doubled. A more extensive Land Purchase Act in 1891 was passed, making thirty-three million pounds available for land purchases. With passage of the Wyndham's Land Act in 1903, the land purchase scheme became widely adopted. It successfully encouraged the sale of entire estates by extending loan money to tenants on advantageous terms and by providing an extra bonus to the landlords if they would comply. In 1909, the Liberal government extended the provisions with the passage of the Birrell's Land Act, finally freeing Irish tenant farmers from the feudal principles on which holding and ownership of land had been based in Ireland for more than two hundred years.

A third Home Rule Bill presented in 1913 passed the House of Commons, but was rejected by the House of Lords. However, under the Parliament Act of 1911 the Lords could only delay legislation. A year later, on September 18, 1914, the Government of Ireland Act received royal assent, but implementation was suspended for the duration of the war. Ulster Unionists in the meantime formed the Ulster Volunteers intending to use force, if necessary, to block a home rule parliament in Ireland. In Dublin, Eoin MacNeill founded the Irish Volunteers as a counter force. Both forces were armed with smuggled weapons. On the political front, Sinn Fein was gaining increased support, breathing new life into the Irish Republican Brotherhood, a secret society originally founded in 1858 during the Fenian movement. A third force, the Irish Citizen army, was organized by labor leader James Connolly.

FROM EASTER REBELLION TO NATIONHOOD

On Easter Monday 1916, a force of fewer than 2,000 insurgents commandeered a number of public buildings in Dublin and proclaimed an

Irish Republic. From the start, the rebellion had no chance of succeeding; the insurgents were under-armed and had inadequate communications, restricting their action essentially to Dublin city. In the aftermath sixteen of the leaders were executed and 3,000 men and women were arrested and interned in prison camps. This heavy-handed response by the British government caused immediate outrage and moved public sympathy to the rebels.

The real backlash, however, came in the 1918 general election when Sinn Fein was swept into office capturing 73 of the 105 Irish seats at Westminster. An invitation went out for all electees to take their seats in an independent national assembly in Dublin. The Sinn Fein members accepted, but only twenty-eight were free to attend as the others were in prison. This group illegally declared a republic, drafted a constitution and created an administrative branch, successfully putting in place a republican infrastructure with alternative courts, police and other institutions.

Britain reinforced its 12,000 constabulary force with almost 40,000 auxiliary and regular military personnel. Irish insurgents mobilized and launched a guerrilla campaign of hit and run warfare for two years. In 1920 nationalists swept all local elections, further weakening the British government's hold over Irish institutions. Following this, Westminster passed a Government of Ireland Act offering limited powers to parliaments representing the six northern and twenty-six southern counties. It was rejected by Sinn Fein and accepted by the Unionists. Subsequent elections were held under this Act in May 1921, which gave Sinn Fein a resounding victory throughout the south, enabling the nationalists to form the second government. This was followed in July of that year by a truce and negotiations that led to the signing of a treaty establishing an Irish Free State with Dominion status in 1922.

THE COLLAPSE OF ASCENDANCY POWER

At the passing of the first Land Act in 1870, only three percent of Irish householders owned their land. By 1916, that figure had grown to almost sixty-four percent, made possible by a radical change in political attitude facilitating the transfer in ownership and making adequate funds available so that tenants could buy their properties outright. The life of wealth and style the landed gentry had enjoyed for two hundred years was finally ending. There was little choice for them as their power and privileges had greatly diminished due to increased burdens brought on by changing economic and political conditions in the nineteenth century. The descendants of families dispossessed in the seventeenth century had come forward to reclaim their ancestral lands.

14

Ascendancy Families of Eastern Connacht

o o o o o o o o o o o o o o o o o o o o o o o o o o o o

Ill fares the land, to hastening ills a prey,
Where wealth accumulates, and men decay:
Princes and lords may flourish, or may fade;
A breath can take them, as a breath has made;
But a bold peasantry, their country's pride,
When once destroyed, can never be supplied.

—Oliver Goldsmith, The Deserted Village

The pace of confiscation and plantation was considerably slower in Connacht (and even more so in the former King's Cantreds) than it was in other parts of Ireland. During the reign of Elizabeth I the Composition of Connacht was introduced in 1585 to provide a new order of land ownership in which title would henceforth be derived from the crown in accordance with English law and not from the Brehon laws of succession as had been the Irish practice. It never became law and was replaced by a series of grants decreed during the reign of James I in the early 1600s, which in fact fulfilled the same objective. Some of these grants went to Tudor and Stuart outsiders, yet in the first half of the seventeenth century many of the influential families were still of Gaelic stock according to known facts extracted from Oliver St John's *Description of Ireland* prepared in 1614:[110]

"The Country of Roscommon had none of the Ancient English (descendants of the Anglo-Normans) races, only a little portion, on the east of the river of Suck, belonging to McDavy one of the Burkes. Of the New English (Tudor settlers or transplanted English) there are Henry Malbye who has the manor of Roscommon; Sir John Kinge who has the Abbey of Boyle; Anthony Brabazon's son who has Ballinste; Sir Thomas LeStrange's heirs who have the lordship of Athleague; and some others seated there since the wars. Of the English transplanted out of the Pale, there are viz. the baron of Delvin and some of the Nugents, Sir Thomas Dillon and divers others. Of the Irishry there is O'Conor Dun, O'Conor Ro, the McDermonds, the O'Kellies; by east of Suck, the O'Hanlies, the O'Flanigans, the Fallons and divers others.

"In Sligo, there are no Ancient or New English. Of transplanted English, Sir William Taffe who has the town and abbey of Sligo and lordship of Ballimot, Nugents and others. Of the Irishry, there are O'Conner Sligo, McDonoghes, O'Hares and some of the McSwynies.

"Leitrim has neither ancient, new or transplanted English. The Irishry are, Orwike (O'Rourke) and those who live under him as the McRannels (Reynolds), the Clan Loughlins, the Clan Murries, the Clan Owens and such others; and McGrannchie who possesses the Dartrie and is a lord himself."

Among the Tudor and Stuart families who settled in Connacht during the reigns of Elizabeth and James I were the Taaffes. Arriving in the early 1600s, they acquired much of the ancestral land of the O'Dowd and MacDonagh clans in County Sligo. The O'Haras of Leyney in County Sligo forfeited some of their ancestral territory in the late sixteenth century to Richard Boyle (later first Earl of Cork), and later interlopers John Crofton and William Clifford succeeded in grabbing additional land from them. To protect what remained of their lands, the O'Haras conformed to the Protestant faith. Henry Ormsby arrived in 1590 and established the family seat in Tubberavaddy near Athleague in County Roscommon. His descendants, siding with the Williamite cause, acquired large quantities of land a century later. The

Mapothers received a large tract of land along the River Shannon in Kilteevan during Elizabeth's reign.

The Kirkwoods of Woodbrook arrived in the early seventeenth century, first settling in County Sligo and later moving to Woodbrook in County Roscommon where they obtained six hundred acres. Greene O'Mulloy, a soldier of fortune with Elizabethan forces in Connacht, acquired considerable property near Roscommon town, and by 1637 the family was in possession of extensive property around Cootehall and Croghan that was previously part of MacDermot ancestral territory. Edward King of Charlestown acquired Dangan Castle and a large tract of land from the O'Beirnes in the early 1600s.

Thomas Wentford, Earl of Stafford, conducted an investigation into County Roscommon lands and their ownership in 1635, and properties found to have title defects were placed with the crown on the basis of an obscure law that gave King Edward IV royal title to Connacht. The dismayed landowners had little choice but to accept the ruling.

In the aftermath of the Cromwellian campaign Connacht's prominent Gaelic families lost most of their ancestral lands when transplantees from other provinces arrived on the scene, asserting their rights to land given to them under the "Hell or to Connacht" edict. Two of the most prominent Connacht families who were dispossessed of their ancestral lands during this period were O'Conor Roe of Ballinafad and MacDermot of Moylurg. Maurice Mahon dispossessed O'Conor Roe along with his tributary septs Hanley and MacBrennan in the reign of Charles II. The King family, already in north Roscommon since 1603, dispossessed the MacDermots of Moylurg of their ancestral lands around Boyle. In other areas of Moylurg the Lamberts, St Georges and Plunkets picked up tracts of MacDermot lands.

The Croftons, a West Yorkshire family, acquired extensive estates throughout counties Roscommon, Leitrim and Sligo. They established the family seat at Moate Park near Roscommon town on lands formally belonging to the Murray family. In 1641, Charles II granted Thomas Lloyd extensive property in Croghan. Following the Cromwellian campaign, Theophilus Sandford was given "all the good lands including the town and castle of Castlerea on the east side of the River Suck" which had belonged to O'Conor Don. The family later purchased additional lands in adjoining townlands.

Donamon Castle and lands in County Roscommon, the seat of the O'Finaghty clan until the thirteenth century, went to the Caulfield family in 1668. The Coopers were granted extensive property in County Sligo and built Markara Castle as the family seat. The Cootes and the Maypowders were granted large tracts of MacDermot Roe and MacManus lands in Kilronan parish. The O'Garas fled to the Continent after the defeat of King James II for whom they had taken up arms.

A few Gaelic families did survive into the Anglo-Irish era. O'Conor Don, after a period of displacement at Kilmactranny in County Sligo, recovered part of his land holdings in the barony of Ballintuber through legal means. MacDermot Roe survived with part of the family's former lands through a grant from Charles II and by conforming during the critical period of the penal laws to the Protestant faith. The O'Haras mentioned above also survived by conforming to the Protestant faith. However, most families forced to relinquish their lands had to content themselves with acreage greatly inferior in size and quality to their earlier possessions.

PROFILES OF TWO ANGLO-IRISH FAMILIES

Unmatched in power and opulence among Connacht's landed families were the Pakenham-Mahons of Strokestown and the Stafford-King-Harmans of Boyle, two of the province's most prominent families. Together they owned more than 80,000 acres when Olive, heiress to the Pakenham-Mahon estate married Edward, heir to the Stafford-King-Harman estate, in 1914. Two years after their marriage the Easter Rising took place, setting in motion a chain of events that led to

Irish independence and with it the twilight of the Anglo-Irish Ascendancy era.

Both the Pakenham-Mahon and Stafford-King-Harman families were distinctively of the Anglo-Irish Ascendancy landed class. Stafford-King-Harman's ancestor, Sir John King of Fethercock Hall, Yorkshire, was given a lease on Boyle Abbey and surrounding lands in compensation for military service to Elizabeth I. He is credited with creating the town of Boyle. In the post-Cromwellian period of Charles II, his descendants were awarded substantial lands belonging to the MacDermots of Moylurg and their tributary families. The family seat was at Boyle until the late 1700s and afterwards at Rockingham on the southeastern side of beautiful Lough Key.

The Pakenham-Mahons (originally Mahon), arriving in Strokestown in the second half of the seventeenth century, were handed a large tract of what had been O'Conor Roe ancestral lands. These lands, confiscated earlier in the Cromwellian conquest, were endowed upon Maurice Mahon in recognition for his services and loyalty to the Royalist cause. The Mahons built their ornate neo-Palladian manor house near the ruins of a pre-historic Firbolg castle and from it ruled a fiefdom that boasted of 27,500 acres and 10,000 tenants by the early 1800s. Throughout the eighteenth century, the Mahons were leading figures in the political and social life of the community. Thomas Mahon (1701–1782) was a leading figure in the Irish House of Commons and he succeeded in marrying his children into some of the leading families of the country. The family became fittingly established when Maurice Mahon was given a peerage in the early 1800s.

The benevolent but autocratic relationship that had existed between the Mahons and their tenants throughout the eighteenth century started to show strain in the years following the end of the Napoleonic Wars in 1815. A stagnant agriculture economy, growth of the rural population and proliferation of tiny tenant farms, mostly on poor soil, alongside large grazing farms of richer soil held by landlords and middlemen, created an atmosphere of hostility and tension. When the

Great Famine of the 1840s hit, tenants on the Mahon estate were among the worst affected by the failure of the potato crop.

The Mahons were among the most active landlords in clearing their lands of tenants, first by assisted passage to Canada, then by random eviction. In 1847 alone, 3,006 tenants were evicted in the Strokestown area, among them one hundred families from the townland of Ballykilcline, "most of whom had been on the land or in the vicinity for an unknown number of generations, some of them apparently since before the conquest."[111] Mahon's was one of several estates where plans were made to colonize the cleared land with Protestant tenants, but there appears to have been little or no responses to ads placed in the Scottish newspapers by Mahon's agent in 1848.[112]

Uneasiness and fear gripped the area as landowners and tenants became terrified of each other: tenants dreading eviction if they could not pay their rent and landlords fearing for their lives. In November of 1847 a rumor spread like wildfire among Mahon's tenants that one of the ships chartered by Mahon to take his tenants to Canada had sunk in the North Atlantic. Retribution was swift: on his way home from a meeting in Roscommon town, Denis Mahon was gunned down by an assailant.

THE EXODUS

The creation of the Irish Free State in 1922 changed forever the political and social environment of the once powerful Anglo-Irish Ascendancy. Many left Ireland taking with them their treasures and leaving behind their "Big Houses," reminders of an era when an oppressed peasantry lived in immense poverty with little or no human dignity afforded them. One by one the houses came tumbling down because they were no longer economically viable to maintain, erasing from Roscommon's landscape the legacy of the once-powerful families. The estate occupied by a succession of Sandfords for 270 years was vacated in 1914 when the last of the Sandfords moved to England. Most of the estate, which in the 1830s had 19,250 acres, was transferred to the tenants in the early part of the twentieth century. The last of the Lloyds of Croghan, John Merrick, died in 1929. Most of the family estate had already passed to the tenants in the early 1900s. Due to financial difficulties the Kirkwoods sold their remaining Woodbrook estate to the Maxwells, a family whose Feely ancestors were land occupiers in the area centuries before the Kirkwoods arrived.

At age 78, Olive Pakenham Mahon bid farewell to her family's ancestral seat at Strokestown Park in 1981. She had lived there all of her life, except for a short period in 1914 when she married Edward Stafford-King-Harman and moved to Rockingham. Olive had returned to her Strokestown family home shortly after Edward was killed in World War I, where she remained for the rest of her life.

The Pakenham-Mahons were eastern Connacht's last Ascendancy family. Olive sold the palatial house and its remaining three hundred acre demesne to local businessman, James Callery, who is characteristic of the new Gaelic-Irish middle-class entrepreneurs that replaced the Anglo-Irish landed gentry. Callery's paternal ancestors had been tenant farmers, some undoubtedly on Pakenham-Mahon lands.

When James Callery bought the "Big House," he came into possession of an extraordinary archive of documents and artifacts from the famine period dealing with the relationship between the Pakenham-Mahons and their tenants. Working from these private papers, Callery and his cousin Luke Dodd (who had returned to Roscommon via Trinity College, Dublin and the Whitney Museum, New York) created a Famine Museum on the Pakenham-Mahon estate dedicated to all tenant farmers who lost their lives through hunger and disease during the horrible famine of the 1840s.

In the words of Ireland's former president, Mary Robinson, patron of the Famine Museum:

> "Every country is quick to make a record of its triumphs. Most cultures are rich in the lore and anecdote that celebrate heroism and strength.... It strikes me how important it is to make a record of a

darker past as well.... More than anything else, this Famine Museum shows us that history is not about power and triumph nearly so often as it is about suffering and vulnerability.... Famine is a central part of our past, a motif of powerlessness which runs through our national consciousness, it is the human drama upon which we, as Irish people, place an enormous value.... We have to wonder again and again at the strength of a people who could survive natural disaster and historic setbacks. As we look at artifacts and open our minds to these stories, we can feel again that it is an Irish strength to celebrate the people in our past, not for power, not for victory, but for the profound dignity of human survival."[113]

Chronology

This is not a complete chronology, but only a list of dates relevant to historical episodes referred to in this book.

c. 7000 B.C.	Beginning of Mesolithic period in Ireland.
c. 3700 B.C.	Neolithic people arrived in Ireland.
c. 2100–1300 B.C.	Building of Irish passage tombs.
c. 1200 B.C.	Arrival of Beaker people.
c. 700 B.C.	Arrival of Priteni tribes (early Celts).
c. 500 B.C.	Euerni Celts colonize Ireland.
c. 300 B.C.	Laginian Celts arrive from Armorica.
c. 150–50 B.C.	Gaels (Milesians) from Spain colonize Ireland.
c. 1–100 A.D.	Gael rulers overthrown by Attacotti.
c. 267 A.D.	King Cormac mac Art dies.
c. 380–405 A.D.	Niall of the Nine Hostages reigns.
358 A.D.	Mugmedon crowned high king of Ireland.
360 A.D.	St. Martin founds first Gallic monastery near Tours.
388 A.D.	King Brian of Connacht dies.
432 A.D.	Pope Celestine sends Patrick to Ireland.
577 A.D.	King Aedh of the *Ui Briuin* dynasty dies.
830 A.D.	Vikings commence settling in Ireland.
1014 A.D.	Battle of Clontarf—Vikings defeated.
1119 A.D.	Turlough Mor O'Conor crowned high king of Ireland.
1156 A.D.	Rory O'Conor succeeds his father as high king of Ireland.

1169 A.D.	Anglo-Normans invade Ireland.
1201 A.D.	Cathal Crobhderg inaugurated king of Connacht at Carnfree.
1224 A.D.	King Henry III grants Anglo-Norman Richard de Burgh most of Connacht.
1224 A.D.	King Henry III retains the Kings Cantreds for himself.
1274 A.D.	Aedh O'Conor, King of Connacht, dies.
1537 A.D.	King Henry VIII assumes title of "King of Ireland."
1558 A.D.	*Compossicion of Connacht* introduced.
1602 A.D.	Battle of Kinsale—Ulster clans defeated.
1609 A.D.	Plantation of Ulster begins under James I.
1641 A.D.	Rebellion by Gaelic/Catholic lords.
1645 A.D.	Cromwell invades Ireland.
1660 A.D.	Restoration of the English monarchy.
1689 A.D.	Battle of the Boyne between William and James II.
1691 A.D.	Treaty of Limerick.
1707 A.D.	"Popery Laws" enacted.
1798 A.D.	Revolutionary uprising by United Irishmen.
1801 A.D.	Union of Ireland and Britain.
1829 A.D.	Catholic Emancipation Act enacted.
1847 A.D.	The Great Famine.
1881 A.D.	First land reform act passed.
1891 A.D.	Land Purchase Act passed.
1909 A.D.	Law freeing tenant farmers from feudal principles.
1916 A.D.	Dublin Rebellion.
1922 A.D.	Twenty-six counties formed into Irish Free State.

Glossary

Ardcarne	Height of the cairn
Bally	Place or farm
Brehon	Judge
Carnfree	Fraioch's cairn
Ceile	Tenant—also plebeian, farmer or rent payer
Celi De	Powerful and puritanical movement in eighth century Ireland
Cinel	Like the clan means descent from a common ancestor
Coarb	Inheritor of a bishopric, or abbacy
Corca	Variation of tribe
Clan	Means children from one common ancestor
Deirbhfine	Loosely applied to any subdivision of society, from the tribe down to the smallest group (such as the family)
Doohie	Variation of tribe
Erenach	Lay manager of monastery and farm
Fili	Poet
Gall	Foreigner
Goidelic	Gaelic or Irish
Gort	Field
Kil	Church
Knock	Hill
Lis	Rampart
Longphort	Chief's fortress
Moylurg	Plain of the tracks of Daghda

Ollamh (Ollav)	Man of learning; poet; doctor
Rath	Fort
Ri tuaithe	Petty king
Roscommon	St. Coman's wood
Sept	A larger group descended from common parents long since dead
Tir	Country
Tribe	Made up of several septs, clans or houses claiming to be descended from a common ancestor
Tuath	Tribe (or territory)

List of Illustrations

1. Map of Contemporary Ireland Showing Counties and Provinces
2. Map of Ireland From Ptolemy's *Geographia*
3. Map of Ireland c. 750 A.D. Showing Major Tribal Groups
4. Map of Ireland Showing Major Dynasties in the Ninth Century
5. Map of Early Historic Ireland
6. Map of Colonial Ireland c. 1240 A.D.
7. Map of Late Fifteenth Century Ireland Showing Territorial Boundaries of Major Clans
8. Map of Ireland Showing Lordships of the Later Middle Ages
9. Map of Thirteenth Century Connacht Showing De Burgh Lordship and the Five Cantreds of the King
10. Map of the County of Roscommon From Scalé's *Hibernian Atlas* (1776)

Bibliography

Bartlett/Jeffery (eds.)   *Military History of Ireland* (Cambridge, 1996)

Barnard, T.C.   *Cromwellian Ireland* (London, 1975)

Becket, J.C.   *The Anglo-Irish Tradition* (London, 1976)

Beirne, Bryan P.   *The Family O'Beirne* (San Francisco, 1997)

Beirne, Francis (ed.)   *The Diocese of Elphin* (Dublin, 2000)

Bottigheimer, Karl S.   *Ireland and the Irish* (New York, 1982)

Bradley, Ian   *The Celtic Way* (London, 1994)

Bulloch, James   *The Life of the Celtic Church* (Edinburgh, 1963)

Burke, Francis   *Loch Ce and its Annals; North Roscommon and the Diocese of Elphin* (Dublin, 1895)

Cahill, Thomas   *How the Irish Saved Civilization* (New York, 1995)

Campbell, Stephen J.   *The Great Irish Famine* (Strokestown, 1994)

Crofton, Francis   *The Story of Mote* (unpublished, 1893)

Cusack, Mary F.   *An Illustrated History of Ireland From A.D. 400 to 1800* (first pub. London, 1868; reissued Guernsey, 1995)

D'Alton, John, Esq.   *King James's Irish Army List, 1689* (special ed. pub. Kansas City, 1997)

D'Alton, John, Esq.   *History of Ireland, Annals of Boyle, Vols. I and II*

De Paor, Liam   *The Peoples of Ireland* (Notre Dame, 1986)

Edwards, Ruth D.   *An Atlas of Irish History* (New York, 1998)

Falley, M. Dickson   *Irish and Scotch-Irish Ancestral Research, Vols. I and II* (Baltimore, 1984)

Flanagan, Laurence   *Ancient Ireland—Life Before the Celts* (New York, 1998)

Freeman, A. Martin (ed.)   *Annala Connachta, 1224–1544* (Dublin, 1944)

French, Maurice	*The Frenches of Frenchpark* (Warminster, UK, 1999)
Gibbon, Skeffington	*Lives and Characters of the Nobility and Gentry of Roscommon* (Dublin, 1829)
Gregory, Lady	*Irish Mythology* (London, 2000)
Grehan, Ida	*The Dictionary of Irish Family Names* (Dublin, 1997)
Harbison, Peter	*Pre-Christian Ireland* (New York, 1988)
Hardiman, James	*History of Galway* (Wombar, HTML Markub 1975)
Hennessy, W.M. (ed.)	*Annals of Loch Ce, Vols. I and II* (Dublin, 1939)
Herm, Gerhard	*The Celts* (New York, 1977)
Hudson, Katherine	*A Royal Conflict* (London 1994)
James, Francis G.	*Ireland and the Empire, 1688–1770* (Cambridge, 1973)
James, Simon	*The Atlantic Celts* (London, 1999)
Jones, Gwyn	*A History of the Vikings* (New York, 1984)
Johnson, Paul	*A History of Christianity* (New York, 1995)
Joyce, P.W.	*A Social History of Ancient Ireland, Vols. I and II* (Kansas City, 1997)
Kilgannon, Tadhg	*Sligo and its Surroundings* (Ballydoogan, 1926)
King, John	*Kingdoms of the Celts* (London, 1998)
King, John	*The Celtic Druids' Year* (London, 1995)
Laing, Lloyd	*Celtic Britain* (New York, 1979)
Lavin, Patrick	*The Celtic World* (New York, 1999)
Lecky, W.E.H.	*A History of Ireland in the Eighteenth Century* (Chicago, 1972)
Lehane, Brendan	*Early Celtic Christianity* (London, 1994)
Lyndon, James	*Ireland in the Later Middle Ages* (Dublin, 1973)
MacLysaght, Edward	*Irish Families, Their Names, Arms and Origins* (Dublin, 1937)
MacManus, Seamus	*The Story of the Irish Race* (New York, 1972)

Bibliography 161

Malcomson, A.P.W.	*John Foster, The Politics of the Anglo-Irish Ascendancy* (Oxford, 1978)
Mattimoe, Cyril	*North Roscommon—Its People and Past* (Boyle, 1992)
McDowell, R.B.	*Ireland in the Age of Imperialism and Revolution 1760–1801* (New York, 1979)
McKenna, Lambert (ed.)	*The Book of O'Hara* (Dublin, 1980)
Moran/Gillespie (eds.)	*Galway: History and Society* (Dublin, 1996)
Mongan, Norman	*The Menapia Quest* (Dublin, 1995)
Moody/Martin (eds.)	*The Course of Irish History* (Cork, 1967)
O'Donovan, John (ed.)	*Annals Of The Kingdom of Ireland by the Four Masters, Vols. I through VII* (Dublin, 1854)
O'Donovan, John	*Tribes and Customs of Hy-Fiachrach [O'Dowda's Country]* (first pub. Dublin, 1844; special ed. pub. Kansas City, 1993)
O'Donovan, John	*Tribes and Customs of Hy-Many [O'Kelly's Country]* (first pub. Dublin, 1843; special ed. pub. Kansas City, 1992
O'Driscoll, Robert (ed.)	*The Celtic Consciousness* (New York, 1981)
O'Hart, John	*Irish Pedigrees or the Origin and Stem of the Irish Nation, Vol. I* (New York, 1923)
O'Rahilly, Thomas F.	*Early Irish History and Mythology* (Dublin, 1946)
O'Rorke, Archd. T.	*History of Sligo—Town and County, Vol. II* (Dublin, 1986)
O'Rorke, Archd. T.	*History, Antiquities and Present State of the Parishes of Ballysadare and Kilvarnet in the County of Sligo* (Dublin)
Otway-Ruthven, A.J.	*A History of Medieval Ireland* (New York, 1993)
Ryan, James G.	*Irish Church Records* (Glenageary, 1992)
Scally, Robert James	*The End of Hidden Ireland* (New York, 1995)
Scherman, Katherine	*The Flowering of Ireland* (Toronto, 1981)
Sharkey, Olive	*Old Days Old Ways* (Dublin, 1994)
Sharkey, P.A.	*The Heart of Ireland* (Dublin, 1927)
Simington, R.C.	*The Transportation of Connacht 1654–1658* (Dublin, 1970)

Simington, R.C.	*Books of Survey and Distribution, County of Roscommon* (Dublin, 1949)
Spellissy, Sean	*The History of Galway* (Limerick, 1999)
Squire, Charles	*Celtic Myths and Legends* (Bath, UK, 2000)
Taylor, J. Sydney (ed.)	*Roscommon Claim to Peerage* (London, 1829)
Weld, Issac	*Statistical Survey of the County of Roscommon* (Dublin, 1832)
Webster, H./Wolf, J.B.	*History of Civilization* (Boston, 1947)
Webster, Richard	*Omens, Oghams & Oracles* (St. Paul, 1995)
Woodham-Smith, Cecil	*The Great Hunger* (New York, 1962)
Roscommon Herald	File copies 1884–1903 (Newspaper Library, London)
Boyle Gazette	File copy, March 14, 1891 (Newspaper Library, London)

About the Author

Patrick Lavin was born in County Roscommon, Ireland. His published books to date are *Arizona: An Illustrated History* (New York, 2001), *The Celtic World: An Illustrated History 700 B.C. to the Present* (New York, 1999), and *Thank You Ireland* (Vancouver, 1994). His work-in-progress is *New Mexico: An Illustrated History*.

Patrick is a graduate of California State University, Northridge, and is retired from service with the United States Government. He lives in Tucson, Arizona.

Endnotes

1. Robert O'Driscoll, ed., *The Celtic Consciousness* (1993)—"Mythology, Literature, and Art" by Proinsias MacCana.
2. Petty kings could do very little to combat Viking attacks, but overlords could provide larger armies. Source: A.J. Otway-Ruthven, *A History of Medieval Ireland* (1993).
3. P.W. Joyce, *A Social History of Ancient Ireland* (1997).
4. Laurence Flanagan, *Ancient Ireland* (1998).
5. Liam De Paor, *The Peoples of Ireland* (1986).
6. Nicholas Wade, "Researchers Trace Roots Of the Irish To Spain," *New York Times*, March 23, 2000.
7. Peter Harbison, *Pre-Christian Ireland* (1988).
8. Also referred to as the Eurerni, Belgic, Menapia and Firbolg.
9. Thomas F. O'Rahilly, *Early Irish History and Mythology* (1946).
10. Ptolemy's *Geography*.
11. *The Menapia Quest* (1995).
12. Thomas F. O'Rahilly, *Early Irish History and Mythology* (1946).
13. The Romans never invaded Ireland.
14. John King, *Kingdoms of the Celts* (1998).
15. *Book of Invasions—source:* Jean Markale, *The Celts* (1993).
16. In Celtic culture, fostering was common. Children would be fostered in the home of a druid, scholar or monk from about the age of seven in order to be educated.

17. Historically, the Fir Bolg, Fir Domnainn and Galiaian can be equated with the Dumnonii of Britain who gave their name to Devon and to the Domnonia in Brittany.
18. Believed to have been derived from the lost work of the *Pytheas of Massalia*, c. 530 B.C., Ptolemy was the earliest known geographer to visit the area.
19. *The Yellow Book of Lecan*—source: Jean Markale, *The Celts* (1993).
20. Translates to *Book of the O'Hara*.
21. Written by Mael-Mura of Othain in 887 A.D.—Source: Thomas F. O'Rahilly, *Early Irish History and Mythology* (1946).
22. Mary Frances Cusack, *An Illustrated History of Ireland* (1995).
23. Thomas F. O'Rahilly, *Early Irish History and Mythology* (1946).
24. Seamus MacManus, *The Story of the Irish Race* (1972).
25. Jean Markale, *The Celts* (1993).
26. *Cumal* was equal to a female slave and she was worth four milk cows.
27. John King, *Kingdoms of the Celts* (1998).
28. Ibid.
29. Ibid.
30. Nigel Pennick, *Celtic Sacred Landscapes* (1996).
31. Ibid.
32. T.W. Moody and F.X. Martin, *The Course of Irish History* (1967).
33. Paul Johnson, *A History of Christianity* (1995).
34. Ibid.
35. John King, *Kingdoms of the Celts* (1998).

36. Devised by Saint Benedict (480–547 A.D.).
37. Translates into Servants of God.
38. Katherine Scherman, *The Flowering of Ireland* (1981).
39. A.J. Otway-Ruthven, *A History of Medieval Ireland* (1993).
40. Ibid.
41. Seamus MacManus, *The Story of the Irish Race* (1972).
42. T.W. Moody and F.X. Martin, *The Course of Irish History* (1967).
43. A.J. Otway-Ruthven, *A History of Medieval Ireland* (1993).
44. Ibid.
45. Ibid.
46. T.W. Moody and F.X. Martin, *The Course of Irish History* (1967).
47. Ibid.
48. Inheritor of a bishopric, abbacy or other ecclesiastical position.
49. Hereditary abbots who were usually tonsured laymen.
50. A.J. Otway-Ruthven, *A History of Medieval Ireland* (1993).
51. James Lydon, *Ireland in the Middle Ages* (1973).
52. From conversations with the late Professor Emeritus B.P. Beirne, Simon Fraser University, British Columbia, Canada.
53. Charles Squire, *Celtic Myths and Legends* (2000).
54. Greek astronomer and geographer from Alexandria.
55. Dermot MacDermot, *MacDermot of Molylurg* (1996).
56. Thomas F. O'Rahilly, *Early Irish History and Mythology* (1946).
57. Tom Cross and Harris Slover, eds., *Ancient Irish Tales* (1996).

58. Taken from *MacDermot of Moylurg* by Dermot MacDermot (1996).
59. Dermot MacDermot, *MacDermot of Moylurg* (1996).
60. Ibid.
61. Henry II, in his settlement of Ireland, had left Rory O'Conor undisputed King of Connacht.
62. Sean Spellissy, *The History of Galway* (1999).
63. Ibid.
64. Ibid.
65. Dermot MacDermot, *MacDermot of Moylurg* (1996).
66. At the time, commodities imported included spices, condiments (like pepper and salt), fruits (such as figs, almonds and raisins), certain finer types of cloths, and other necessities.
67. Sean Spellissy, *The History of Galway* (1999).
68. Ibid.
69. O'Hanley.
70. Much has been penned to commemorate the fame and distinction of the Three Tuaths and their ruling families down the ages such as this verse.
71. P.W. Joyce, *A Social History of Ireland* (1997).
72. Bagna may have been the name of a Firbolgan chieftain that ruled the area.
73. Translated means "people of the sons of Eric."
74. Dermot MacDermot, *MacDermot of Moylurg* (1996).
75. Ibid.
76. P.A. Sharkey, *Heart of Ireland* (1927).

77. The building of this great church is recorded in the *Annals of the Four Masters* as having occurred in 1151–1152. A seemingly related entry in the *Annals* for 1176 describes how King Roderic O'Conor granted land in the townland of Toomaghy as a perpetual gift to "God and Saint Berach" in exchange for "sureties" from Archbishop Kewyley O'Duffy, Flann O'Finnaghty, Hugh O'Flynn, Rourke O'Mulrenin, Ignatius O'Monaghan, O'Hanly, Conor MacDermot and others. The "sureties" were a form of concomitant or promise under Brehan law to a king when he donated land to the founder of a monastery, the custom in Ireland at the time.

78. John O'Donovan *Letters Containing Information Relative to the History and Antiquities of Co. Roscommon, Collected During the Progress of the Ord. Survey, 1836–37* (Bray, 1927).

79. Dermot MacDermot, *MacDermot of Moylurg* (1996).

80. Stanleys were an old English family.

81. *Annals of Lough Ce*, *Annals of Connaght* and the *Annals of the Four Masters*.

82. William M. Hennessy (ed.), *Annals of Lough Ce* (1939).

83. John O'Donovan's *Letters* (Bray, 1927).

84. Translated means "Church of the Mounds." A graveyard, still in use, is where this church was located.

85. There are many variants of this name, but the modern versions are given as O'Mulvihill and O'Mulvey.

86. John O'Donovan's *Letters* (Bray, 1927).

87. P.W. Joyce, *A Social History of Ancient Ireland* (1997).

88. Ibid.

89. Source: *Book of Armagh*, as translated by Liam De Paor (1993).

90. From whom the name MacBranan evolves.

91. Francis Beirne, ed., *The Diocese of Elphin* (2000).
92. Ibid.
93. Hereditary abbots who were usually tonsured laymen.
94. P.A. Sharkey, *The Heart of Ireland* (1927).
95. John Donovan *Letters* (Bray, 1927).
96. MacFirbis gave them a spurious descent from the *Ui Briuin na Sionna*.
97. Great-grandfather of *Conchobhar* from whom the O'Conors of Connacht derive their name.
98. Located in present day Counties Dublin and Meath.
99. *Topographical Poems of John O'Dubhagain*, c. 1320.
100. *Four Masters* and *Loch Ce*.
101. Taken from *The Family O'Beirne* (1997) by permission of the author, Dr. Brian Beirne.
102. Martin A. Freeman (ed.), *Annals of Connacht* (1944).
103. King of the adjoining kingdom of Moylurg.
104. Dr. B.P. Beirne, *The Family O'Beirne* (1997).
105. Ibid.
106. Liam De Poar, *The Peoples of Ireland* (1986).
107. Meaning those who did not conform to the Protestant Anglican religion.
108. Edmund Curtis, *History of Medieval Ireland, 1086–1513* (1938). Source: A.J. Otway-Ruthven, *A History of Medieval Ireland* (1993).
109. His ancestor was High King when the Normans invaded Ireland in 1169.

110. *A Description of Ireland* (1614) by Oliver St John (Carew MSS VI p. 294), extracted from *The MacDermots of Moylurg* (1996).
111. Robert Scally, *The End of Hidden Ireland* (1995).
112. Stephen J. Campbell, *The Great Irish Famine* (1994).
113. Ibid (from the Preface).

Index

A

Act of Union 138, 139
Ailill 14, 65, 66, 67
Airtech 64, 90
Amalgaid 67
Anglican 102, 114, 120, 129, 170
Anglo-Norman xvii, 52, 54, 55, 58, 59, 63, 69, 75, 76, 78, 79, 80, 82, 83, 102, 113, 125, 129, 146, 154
Annaghmare 5
Armagh 5, 39, 40, 56, 169
Assicus 112
Athy 81
Attacotti 27, 65, 153
Aughrim 89, 119, 126
Augustinian Canons 113
Auterii 64

B

Badgna 111
Ballyfeeny 99
Balor 18, 19
Bel 37
Belgae xiii, 12, 13, 14, 15, 18, 64
Black death 57
Blake 81
Bodkin 81
Boyle xi, 68, 90, 117, 120, 146, 147, 148, 149, 159, 161, 162
Boyne 6, 15, 133, 134, 154
Brehon Code 83, 92, 99, 124
Brian xi, xvi, 47, 50, 51, 66, 67, 89, 90, 97, 102, 115, 116, 123, 153, 170
Brian Boru xvi, 50, 51, 97
Britain xiii, xvii, 5, 7, 11, 12, 13, 14, 21, 25, 27, 38, 40, 137, 143, 154, 160, 166
Brittany 6, 12, 166
Brougham 105
Brown 26, 81

Bruce 58
Bumlin 97, 105, 109
Burke 113, 159

C

Cairbre 28, 105, 123
Callery xi, 127, 151
Callraighe 91, 110
Calraige 64, 91
Canada xi, 150, 167
Canterbury 56
Carbri Cinn Cait 27
Carlos 117
Carn Froach 68
Carrowkeel 5, 6
Carrowmore 6
Cashel 15, 42, 48, 56
Celi De 41, 42, 155
Celtic xi, xiii, xiv, xv, xvii, xviii, 4, 7, 11, 12, 15, 16, 17, 21, 25, 30, 32, 35, 36, 37, 38, 40, 41, 42, 51, 55, 63, 89, 133, 159, 160, 161, 162, 163, 165, 166, 167
Celts xiii, xvii, 3, 7, 11, 12, 14, 15, 16, 17, 35, 37, 64, 89, 99, 153, 159, 160, 165, 166
Cenel MacErca 89
Charles I 131, 132, 147, 148, 149
Ciarrage 64
Clonmacnoise 16, 42
Clontarf xvi, 50, 51, 97, 153
Cloonfinlough 109
Compossicion of Connacht 83, 124, 154
Conchobar 14, 115
Conn 21, 27, 28, 29, 48, 66, 115, 116
Connacht xiii, xvi, xvii, xviii, 4, 5, 14, 19, 27, 29, 51, 54, 55, 56, 57, 59, 63, 64, 65, 66, 67, 68, 69, 75, 76, 77, 78, 79, 80, 82, 83, 84, 85, 87, 88, 89, 91, 92, 97, 100, 102, 104, 109, 110, 114, 116, 117, 119, 121, 124, 125, 127, 133, 145,

146, 147, 148, 151, 153, 154, 157, 161, 168, 170
Connachta 29, 159
Connolly 142
Cooley 14, 65
Cootehall 147
Corca Eachlin xvii, xviii, 88, 89, 97, 103, 109, 110, 111, 116, 117, 119
Cork 48, 57, 146, 161
Cormac Mac Airt 66
Costello 71
Cox 105, 107
Crofton 122, 124, 146, 159
Cromwell 125, 131, 132, 154
Cruachan 66, 68
Cruthin 65
Cu Chulainn 65

D

Daire 13, 65
Daithi 66, 67
Dal Cais 49
Dal-Riada 13, 14
Dana 18
Darcy 81
Dark Ages xv, 40, 41, 63
De Burgh 76, 77, 78, 79, 80, 81, 82, 85, 92, 154, 157
De Exeter 77
Deane 81
Deirbhfine 30, 31, 155
Denmark xvi, 49
Desmond 58
Dodd xi, 151
Dofa xvii, xviii, 88, 89, 97, 98, 99, 100, 102, 103, 104, 105, 109, 117, 119
Dowth 6
Druid 36, 111, 165
Druidism xiv, 35, 36, 37, 38, 113
Dublin xvi, 4, 14, 28, 42, 47, 48, 49, 52, 56, 57, 59, 98, 113, 130, 131, 134, 135, 138, 140, 141, 142, 143, 151, 154, 159, 160, 161, 162, 170

E

Edward III 80

Edward IV 147
Egyptians 19
Eire 13
Elphin 69, 88, 101, 109, 110, 113, 114, 117, 120, 122, 124, 126, 127, 159, 170
Euerni 13, 153
Europe xiii, xv, 4, 7, 11, 12, 20, 40, 41, 43, 56, 57, 58, 82, 136, 139

F

Feeny 99
Fenian 142
Fiachra 66, 67, 68
Finn MacCool 28
Fir Domnainn 18, 166
Firbolg xiii, 14, 19, 26, 64, 88, 90, 109, 120, 149, 165
Fitzgerald 52, 59, 77
Font 81
Formorian 19
France 3, 6, 41, 53, 59, 82, 83, 132, 133, 137
French 53, 81, 83, 126, 160

G

Gaelic xv, xvi, xvii, xviii, 4, 12, 18, 30, 50, 53, 54, 58, 59, 60, 76, 79, 80, 81, 83, 84, 89, 92, 93, 97, 99, 102, 109, 116, 117, 123, 124, 125, 126, 129, 130, 131, 133, 136, 145, 147, 148, 151, 154, 155
Gaels xvii, xviii, 12, 15, 19, 20, 27, 49, 54, 58, 63, 76, 79, 105, 153
Galioin 14, 64
Galloglasses 58, 76
Galway xi, 18, 28, 40, 64, 75, 77, 80, 81, 82, 83, 92, 160, 161, 162, 168
Gaul xiii, 5, 7, 11, 12, 13, 15, 21, 25, 30, 35, 39, 41
Gillstown 99, 105
Golden Age xv
Gowanree 88, 89
Gregraige 64
Guaire 67

H

Hallstatt 11, 16
Hebrides 19, 50

Henry II xvi, 52, 54, 58, 69, 77, 78, 88, 92, 118, 154, 168
Henry III 77, 78, 92, 154
Henry IV 78, 92
Henry VIII 60, 102, 114, 130, 131, 154

I

Iberia 11, 12, 15
Ice Age 3, 4, 57
Iron Age xiv, 11, 15, 25, 35
Isle of Man 50

J

James I 131, 132, 145, 146, 148, 154
James II 132, 148, 154
Jocelin 112
John 16, 37, 58, 77, 87, 98, 101, 102, 103, 104, 110, 113, 117, 119, 126, 127, 145, 146, 149, 151, 159, 160, 161, 165, 166, 169, 170, 171
Joyce 81, 111, 160, 165, 168, 169

K

Kells 70, 101, 113, 117
Kerry 15
Kilbarry 69, 98, 106, 107
Kilcline 99
Kilgefin 97
Kilglass 97, 99, 101, 102, 104, 105, 106, 107, 108, 119, 126
Kilkenny 59, 131
Kilmore 89, 106, 119, 122, 124, 126
Kiltrustan 105, 109
Kinel Dofa xvii, xviii, 88, 89, 97, 98, 99, 100, 102, 103, 104, 105, 117, 119
Kinvara 67
Knowth 5, 6

L

La Tene 11, 13, 16, 40
Laginian 14, 64, 153
Lake Arrow 6
Lambay 47
Lavagh 99, 106
Leinster 14, 15, 27, 28, 29, 51, 52, 59, 88
Limerick 48, 50, 70, 71, 134, 154, 162

Lindisfarne 40, 47
Lios-a-Duirn 122
Lloyd 147, 160
Loch Owel 49
Longford 50, 105
Lough Boderg 99, 119
Lough Lagan 105, 106, 107, 108
Lugaid 13
Lugh 19
Lynch 81, 113

M

MacBranan 70, 103, 169
MacBrennan xi, 90, 109, 110, 114, 115, 116, 117, 147
MacDermot 63, 68, 70, 91, 103, 122, 123, 124, 147, 148, 167, 168, 169
MacDermot Roe 148
MacDockwra 70
MacEgan 70
MacMaon 91
MacMurrough 51, 52, 59
MacNeill 142
MacRannall 103
MacShane 105, 106, 107, 108
MacTully 70
MacWilliam Lower 80
MacWilliam Upper 80
Mageraghty 69, 70, 71
Malachy 49, 51
Mannachan 90, 120
Martin 25, 39, 81, 153, 159, 161, 166, 167, 170
Mayo 5, 6, 18, 64, 80, 90, 141
McGreevy 64, 91, 92, 110
Meath 5, 14, 20, 27, 29, 36, 49, 67, 70, 71, 88, 133, 134, 170
Menappi 14
Milesians 12, 15, 18, 153
Mongfionn 66
Morris 81
Moses 19, 20
Mount Sandel 4
Moylurg 57, 63, 64, 68, 70, 77, 90, 91, 92, 103, 110, 122, 123, 147, 149, 155, 168, 169, 170, 171
Moytura 18, 19

Mug Nuadat 21
Mugmedon 66, 153
Mulrooney 68, 91, 92, 110
Munster 14, 20, 28, 50, 51, 77, 107, 131

N

Neary 101
Neolithic xiii, 4, 5, 6, 13, 153
Niall of the Nine Hostages 29, 153
Norse xvi, xvii, 49, 50, 56
Norway xv, 47, 49, 58

O

O'Beirne 69, 70, 89, 90, 109, 113, 119, 121, 122, 123, 124, 125, 126, 159, 170
O'Birn 122, 123, 124
O'Cleary 127
O'Concannon 69
O'Conor xvi, 51, 52, 53, 68, 70, 71, 75, 76, 77, 78, 79, 80, 81, 84, 92, 97, 102, 103, 104, 110, 114, 115, 116, 118, 120, 122, 123, 124, 146, 147, 148, 149, 153, 154, 168, 169
O'Conor Don 84, 102, 103, 124, 148
O'Conor Roe 102, 103, 104, 115, 116, 147, 149
O'Conor Sligo 102
O'Donnell 114, 131
O'Dowd 146
O'Duffy 113, 117, 118, 169
O'Fallon 69
O'Farrell 102, 120
O'Finaghty 69, 70, 71, 148
O'Flaherty 70, 80, 81
O'Flannagan 69, 70, 71
O'Flynn 69, 70, 169
O'Gara 14, 70
O'Grady 101
O'Hanly 169
O'Hara 14, 70, 161, 166
O'Heyne 69
O'Kelly 64, 70, 161
O'Malley 70
O'Monaghan 89, 90, 119, 120, 121, 122, 169
O'Mulconroy 69, 70, 127
O'Mullaly 113
O'Mulloy 147
O'Mulrenin 69, 70, 71, 169
O'Mulvihill 110, 169
O'Neill 49, 131
O'Reilly 70
O'Rourke 52, 70, 146
O'Shaughnessy 69
O'Shield, Connacht 114
O'Teighe 69
Oilill Olum 64
Olaf 48, 49
Ona 89, 110, 111, 112, 113, 114
Osmonde 58

P

Pakenham-Mahon 148, 149, 151
Paleolithic 3
Parnell 140, 141
Patrick, Saint 28, 37, 38, 69, 110, 111, 112, 113, 114, 119
Picti 13
Picts 19
Portugal 83
Prendergast 77
Prince John 77
Priteni 12, 153
Ptolemy 9, 13, 18, 64, 157, 165, 166

Q

Queen Maeve 6, 19

R

Rathcroghan 65
Reformation 38, 101, 102, 113, 130
Richard II 59, 81, 83
Robinson, Mary 151
Roman xv, xvi, 11, 12, 15, 25, 30, 38, 39, 41, 101
Rome 12, 41, 55, 121, 130
Roscommon xi, 57, 64, 66, 68, 70, 77, 88, 92, 95, 103, 116, 119, 125, 146, 147, 148, 150, 151, 156, 157, 159, 160, 161, 162, 163, 169

S

Samhain xiv, 36

Sandford 84, 148
Scotia 20
Scotland 4, 6, 19, 40, 47, 58, 59, 76
Shanley 107
Shannon xi, xviii, 19, 27, 29, 49, 57, 63, 67, 77, 78, 88, 90, 97, 105, 111, 119, 126, 147
Sil Murray 64, 68, 70, 90, 91, 92, 98, 116, 117
Sinn Fein 142, 143
Sitric 49
Skerrett 81
Slieve Bawn 89
Sligo xi, 5, 6, 14, 19, 26, 64, 77, 92, 102, 109, 114, 146, 147, 148, 160, 161
Sogain 65
Spain 3, 12, 19, 20, 83, 104, 153, 165
Spanish peninsula 83
Stauntons 77
Stone Age 3, 5
Strokestown 105, 109, 148, 149, 150, 151, 159
Strongbow 52
Stuart 133, 145, 146

T

Tadhg of the Towers 91
Tara 15, 27, 28, 48, 66, 67
Termonbarry 97, 105
Three Tuaths xvii, 77, 88, 89, 90, 92, 93, 97, 109, 119, 168
Tir Briuin 119, 121, 124, 126
Tir-Briuin-na-Sionna xvii, xviii, 88, 89, 97, 105, 109, 119
Tir-Tuathail 90
Tribes of Galway 81

Tuam 56, 66, 118, 127
Tuatha de Danann 17, 18, 91
Tuathal Feachtmar 27
Tuathal Techmar 27
Tudor 80, 124, 130, 132, 133, 134, 145, 146
Turgeis 49
Turlough Mor 68, 69, 153
Tyrone 67

U

Ui Aillela 67
Ui Briuin xiii, 29, 67, 68, 79, 89, 90, 91, 153, 170
Ui Briuin Ali 67, 68
Ui Briuin Seola 67
Ui Fiachra 67, 68, 91
Ui Maine 64, 65
Ui Neill 29, 67
Uisneach 36
Ulaid 15
Ulster 4, 6, 13, 14, 20, 29, 40, 50, 56, 65, 80, 84, 125, 131, 141, 142, 154
United Irishmen 126, 137, 138, 154

V

Victoria, Queen 127
Vikings xv, xvi, 47, 48, 49, 50, 91, 97, 153, 160

W

Wales 52, 53
Waterford 48, 50
Wexford 48, 50
William of Orange 132
Williamite War 104, 125, 129, 130, 133

0-595-26477-8

Printed in the United Kingdom
by Lightning Source UK Ltd.
98533BA/8